Seams to Me

24 New Reasons to Love Sewing

by Anna Maria Horner

WILEY

Wiley Publishing, Inc.

WILEY

Acquisitions Editor
Roxane Cerda

Project Editor
Donna Wright

Editorial Manager
Christina Stambaugh

Publisher
Cindy Kitchel

Vice President and Executive Publisher
Kathy Nebenhaus

Interior Art Director
Tai Blanche

Cover Design
Susan Olinsky

Photography
Anna Maria Horner

Page Layout
Erin Zeltner

Graphics Technicians
Joni Burns
Nikki Gately
Ronda David-Burroughs
Brent Savage

This book is lovingly dedicated to my mother, Mary Lynn. Her gentle spirit, cheerful presence and clever hands inspire more than she'll ever know. Every day in my life is another chance to live up to her example.

Acknowledgments

I am so honored to count Jennifer and Joelle Hoverson of purlsoho.com as my good friends and thankful for their generosity in supplying all the fabrics for this book.

My dear sweet pal, Tracy Smith offered her welcoming Tennessee farmhouse, complete with several charming animals (adorable children too!) all to prove that she is the best cheering section a girl could have. So many photographs in this book are beautiful because of the world she lives in, and I am thankful that she shares it with me.

Everyone should know a man as kind and pleasant as Mr. Jack Freeman. His talent on the mandolin is only exceeded by the coolness of his 1940's Ford pickup. I am so glad he takes requests on both.

The folks at Bread & Company of Nashville were so generous in letting us stand and admire their pastry case long enough to get some beautiful photographs. We got a few delicious pistachio macaroons and a cheesecake, too.

I'd like to thank the following beauties for their patience in letting me sprinkle their faces on the pages of this book: Tracy, Ali, and Hannah Smith; Hannah Daniel; Louise Bacon; Eleni Nine; Cece McKennon; Juliana, Nicolas, Joseph, Isabela, and Eleni Horner; and King Leo the world's cutest yellow lab.

And thank you to my incredibly supportive and patient husband, Jeff, who knew when to push me towards my manuscript and when to drag me away from it (even if I fought him every time). Our whole family hums happier because of his love and care.

24 New Reasons to Love Sewing

Part 1 Getting Started

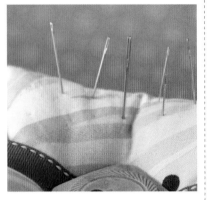

Part 2 Projects

Organize

6

Stylize

7

Decorate

8

Domesticate

9

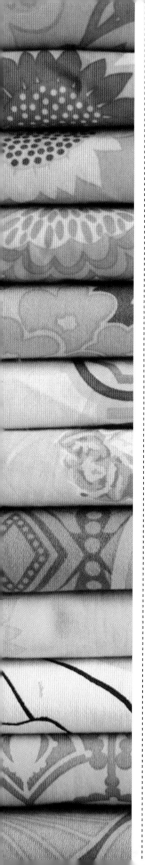

Introduction

I smell a newly purchased cotton fabric getting toasty under the steam of a good pressing, and I am immediately back in the basement of my childhood home with my bare feet nestled between the fibers of the green shag carpet, where the same smell told me my new dress was almost done. I watch my littlest ones dashing through bolts at the local fabric shop and reminisce of hiding in that dream-world with my sister as Mom gazed up to the right, head tilted to the left, calculating yardage in her mind. She was so careful to not overbuy. The taste of embroidery floss against my tongue as I ready it to pass through the needle's eye invites me up on my lofty little-girl bed where I taught myself to make my first French knot when I was 8 years old. Each near miss of the sewing machine's needle when I dare my fingers a bit too close, convincing the fabric to go my way, brings to mind the equally painful and humorous occasion of Mom manually turning the machine's wheel in reverse to remove the needle from my middle finger. I cried until I laughed, she laughed until she cried and then we kept sewing. And the sound of my oldest daughter stitching away at her end of the sewing table assures me that I won't soon lose any of these most perfect memories that speak to every sense. These recollections seam together my past, my present, and my future.

Setting out to write this book was an exhilarating yet daunting task for someone who would rather just invite you here for the day to show you how to make something. My greatest hope for this collection of projects, ideas, tips, and tutorials is that you'll feel as though you have indeed been here and also that you want to come back. And who are you, anyway? I think perhaps you are green as a cucumber and need some friendly advice and a few simple projects to get you inspired. I think maybe you know how to sew a little but want something to gel together all your existing skills and experiences. I suspect also that you could probably teach me a thing or two, but appreciate interesting ideas in the form of charming clothing and accessories, clever house goods, and well-worn techniques. Welcome to you all! I hope you learn something that you'll teach to someone else. And my most personal wish is that you will love sewing more than you did before.

This book is divided generally into two parts. Part I includes everything from identifying essential tools to walking around the color wheel. We begin by understanding all the ideal components of a sewing space and get a glimpse at the most practical and useful tools for measuring, cutting, pressing, and sewing. I've offered what I hope to be an insightful look at how to buy a sewing machine, what types of needles, pins, and thread to use and when, and an overview of the ominous notions category. Near and dear to my textile-designing heart is Chapter 3, where I've helped you explore textiles with your mind before you do it on foot. I've even cooked up "color recipes" to help you choose and combine print, color, and pattern all based on color theory. Also very useful are the definitions of all those tedious fabric terms to decipher the lingo at the cutting counter. Chapters 4 and 5 wrap up this part with a series of tutorials, both at the machine and by hand, that will be referred back to several times throughout the projects in this book. Nesting them all together, one after the other, also makes them easily referenced later on in your everyday sewing.

Part II includes 24 projects divided in to four categories: Organize, Stylize, Decorate, and Domesticate. This collection of projects was simply inspired by what I find myself wanting to make in these categories. Many of the projects have corresponding pattern pages for you to cut out and others list the specific dimensions to use or show you how to make a pattern based on specific measurements. The projects range from simple to complex, which I hope offers something for everyone no matter your skill level. Several are for function, several are for fun, and most of them are for both. There are projects that echo my love of patchwork. There are projects that I've put together on paper for the first time, though I've been sewing them freestyle for myself and my family for years. And there are projects ideal for giving and for keeping. What I really hope is that what you choose to keep will be passed on for generations.

It seems to me that the best thing that ever happened in those fabrics stores in the 70s was that Mom did overbuy every now and then. Perhaps after a while, responding to my dabbling, she did so on purpose. And somewhere along the way as I learned to make things, I also learned to love the very process of making them just as much. It seems to me that our everyday needs can be answered with more than just the store-bought. It seems to me that our hands can be used for more than just the keyboard. It seems to me that I'm not the only one who thinks this way, and I'm glad you're here.

xo

Anna Maria

Please check out my dedicated Flickr group to share your *Seams to Me* project photos. Visit annamariahorner.blogspot.com for more details.

Part 1 Getting Started

Chapter 1

Room to Sew

Whether sewing is new to you or not, one of the greatest challenges in home sewing is finding the right space and stocking it. If you're just beginning, it's likely that you will amass over time gadgets, tools, and a

fabric stash with each new project that you tackle. To get you started, I will discuss the sewing must-haves or basic items that you will need and how to create a functional and enjoyable sewing space.

Finding the Perfect Perch

Do you have a 500-square-foot studio? Great! You only have a spare bedroom? Perfect! What did you say, a mere corner in the laundry room? Oooo, cozy! Just the dusty floor of a coat closet? That'll do; get the broom and let's get to work!

Well, Look at You!

If you are one of the lucky ones who have an entire room in your house dedicated to your sewing, first be very thankful. Right after that, think about your space. You'll need three main centers of function—a place to do your folding and cutting (a roomy table or counter), a place to do your pressing (an ironing board), and a spot to do your sewing (the sewing machine area). This trio is best arranged in a "U" formation, whether you have a small or very spacious room.

I've sewn in every type of environment that I've listed so far, and am still learning what works best. I've had a mere closet, and I've had an 1,800-square-foot studio/boutique. In all instances, I've enjoyed the process of making the most of it, and it has always involved using some found furniture or storage.

Whether it's the sewing table, the chair, the shelves, the cutting table, or whatever else you're on the hunt for, repurposing old garage sale or estate sale furniture into something useful can be very rewarding. It just takes a little creativity and brainpower to take the place of the dollars you would otherwise spend on all-new pieces. Talk to people you know who sew, and ask what setup works for them and why. It can sometimes take professionals years to get their sewing space the way they want it. Like any designing in your home, it is not an overnight process, but a personal journey to a place you may end up liking best of all.

Pull Up a Chair

Setting your sewing machine on a standard-height dining table and sitting yourself in a standard-height dining chair will put you too low to sew comfortably. You don't want to be reaching up to sew, nor do you want to be reaching down. Neither of these options is good for the back, neck, or shoulders. It's also not good for your project results!

For a test to see if your chair-and-table setup is ideal, you could try the following: put your machine on the table and sit in the chair right up to it; with your upper arms relaxed down to your sides, raise up your forearms so that they are bending at a perfect perpendicular angle toward the machine; then flex back your wrists a bit so that your hands can rest comfortably on the extension table or near the needle plate (which is the flat part of the machine where your fabric runs across). If you have to hunch up your shoulders to do this, or are raising your elbows up quite a bit, you are most likely sitting too low. Find a suitable chair, like a rolling, adjustable office chair, and be the high-and-mighty seamstress you always wanted to be.

Creative Control Station

For those of you that have a corner in a room where you can leave your sewing setup intact around the clock, you can think of your space as a workstation. You would likely want to employ some space-saving measures within your workstation and have most everything you need during your sewing time within arm's reach. There are countless all-in-one sewing-table arrangements in the marketplace in a range of prices, much like computer stations, that are ideal for this situation. Many of these sewing stations have folding table extensions for cutting your fabrics, and shelves or drawers underneath for storing supplies.

This may seem obvious but, if you take the plunge and buy a sewing center, *sit at it first!* There are poorly designed sewing tables out there that barely leave room for your legs when you are sitting at the machine. You'll never sit dead-center in front of a sewing machine; you'll sit center-left in front of the needle of the sewing machine. So test it in the store and make sure that you are comfortable and you have enough leg room. Because of this, I wouldn't recommend buying a sewing center or sewing cabinet online or from a catalog, unless they can guarantee returns.

See What I Mean?

Natural sunlight is a glorious and perfect (and free) light in which to sew, as well as to do your pinning and cutting. That doesn't mean that you can sew only during the day. Pfiff! You may be burning the midnight oil, but one little ceiling fixture won't do. This is true for either nighttime or daytime sewing.

A lighting expert would suggest that you have at least 150 watts of incandescent or 40 watts of fluorescent light for all the tasks in your sewing projects. This should be shaded light, not bare bulbs shining in your eyes. Try to situate the lighting around your sewing

machine area so that it's not casting shadows where you are working. If you have the table or the floor space nearby, an adjustable arm lamp is a good way to get the light situated just where you need it.

There are all types of special sewing lights available, but it's not a must. If you have special needs concerning your vision, absolutely make that a priority and get the advice of your eye doctor as well. Especially for hand sewing, there are many light and magnifier combinations on the market to make your sewing time more comfortable on the eyes. Some lights will help you see color more accurately when you are matching cloth to thread as well.

Color Me Happy

Talking about light also means talking about color. Yes, indeed. Lighter shades on the walls will be more reflective and provide more surrounding light. The same applies to every last surface of the whole room. The floor will be more reflective if it's wood or some other slick surface, rather than carpet, especially a light-colored, slick surface.

The color of your sewing space is as personal a decision as the fancy fabrics you choose for your sewing projects. Most of all, it needs to make you happy. If there is any spot in the house that you want to get a little kooky-creative with, this is the place to play. If you are set on a deep wall color, perhaps apply it to only one wall and not the wall by your sewing machine.

The Sewing Machine

Choosing a sewing machine is a very weighted decision for some, but not something that should be a drag or difficult. My first machine was 30 years old by the time it was all mine, and I made countless things on that old faithful friend. I've sewn on all kinds of machines from several different manufacturers. Everyone has a different opinion about what brand to go with or how many bells and whistles should be ringing and singing when you sew. You should think of the perfect machine as being an extension of you. The best machine for you is the one that keeps you inspired to try new things but doesn't overwhelm you. Therefore, making this decision is a completely personal one, which is why I am not endorsing any particular sewing machine in this book. But let's chat about some things to consider before you purchase one.

Bobbin' Around a Sewing Machine

If you've never sewn before or are very new to sewing, it's helpful to have a handle on the general layout of a basic machine before you start shopping for your own or test-driving them. Every machine will vary to a certain degree. If you've just bought a machine, it should come with a detailed user's manual. Never buy one without it. Below is a general image guide to a machine, followed by a list and description of its parts. Keep in mind that some of the settings shown as a knob on this diagram may be adjusted through an LCD screen on a computerized machine.

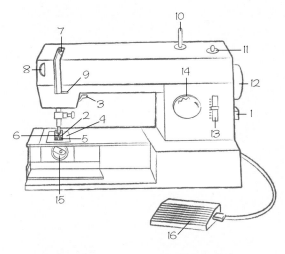

1	Power switch	9	Thread guide
2	Presser foot	10	Spool pin
3	Presser foot lifter	11	Bobbin winder
4	Throat plate	12	Balance wheel
5	Feed dogs	13	Stitch length regulator
6	Needle	14	Stitch width regulator
7	Thread take-up	15	Bobbin case/bobbin
8	Upper tension regulator	16	Foot control

A lifetime of sewing will most likely involve more than one machine. So if you can make a healthy investment, stitch quality and user-friendliness are hallmarks of what to look for. A great machine should last for decades.

Ask Yourself This

You should begin your sewing machine hunt by asking yourself some questions. It might be a good idea to write your answers to these questions to help you formulate what you'll be looking for.

- What kind of items will I be making? Quilting, garments, or both?
- What kind of fabrics do I want to sew with?
- What is my budget?
- How often will I use the machine?
- Do I want to start a home-based sewing business?
- Am I a beginner, experienced, or expert seamstress?
- Will I need/want to upgrade as I become more experienced?

Shop It

Just like bringing home any other type of technology or appliance, it's always good to read consumer reviews. If your friends and family sew, ask them what they sew on, and then do an online search on those models. Or ask to try out a friend's machine before you take the plunge yourself. Many sewing magazines offer product reviews in an annual issue or on the magazine's Web site when the new models debut.

Like everything else, you'll have several choices of machines for sale online, in fabric stores, in department stores, and through local dealers. Of all these choices, I can't really advise buying a machine online, unless you've already had a chance to test-sew with the exact same model. Even so, every machine is unique, just like a car, and they all have personalities, even when you're buying high-end.

The single most important rule I would offer about buying any sewing machine, no matter how much you spend, is *sew on it as much as you can before buying it*. You must love the way it sews or at least be comfortable with how it feels, even if it's a lower-end model. Call ahead and find out a non-busy time to visit the store or dealer. Bring in your own fabric scraps, thread, trims, and anything else you want to cart into the store. If they say you can't use your own materials or that you can sew on it only for a minute or two, then that should be your last verbal exchange on your way out the door. Let the salesperson show you every feature possible, even the buttonhole feature. Then do not be afraid to try everything out yourself. Twice.

Going in for the Buy

The machine is obviously going to be the biggest single investment in your sewing world. So while you shouldn't stress over it, you shouldn't take it lightly, either, especially if you are spending more than a few hundred dollars. If you are spending less than that, you may consider buying a used machine from a dealer, especially if it comes with a locally based warranty or trade-in value. It isn't a bad way to get started. There is nothing wrong with spending only $100 on a brand-new machine at your local discount store—just don't expect much. It may be the perfect thing to get you started on simple projects, but your skill level will eventually exceed what it can do for you in terms of stitch quality and dependability. The opposite would also be true. It may be foolish to have a payment plan for an $8,000 machine that completely exceeds your skill level and needs.

If you are shy and don't feel like you know how to negotiate well, take an experienced sewing friend with you, to help out. In fact, take this book with you. There are advantages to going to a local dealer, such as having access to a repair shop or a chance to upgrade later, classes on your new machine or on learning how to expand your equipment attachments, meeting other people who love sewing, and having an actual face to talk to when something goes wrong. Your machine should always come with at least basic manufacturer's warranty, but it's up to you whether you feel more comfortable purchasing additional warranties.

No One Likes Bad Press

When you're sewing that snazzy stuff, you should be using an iron just about as much as you use your sewing machine, possibly even more. Every single line of stitching that you make should be pressed at one point, and usually before the item is even finished. So, you need to consider setting up a place for pressing near your sewing area. If you don't already own an iron and ironing board that you're happy with, you may want to add these items to your shopping list.

Note: Before you press, always test a little unused corner of your fabric first, for the right heat and process.

The Iron

Who loves to iron? No hands raised? Agreed. Well, you actually don't have to *iron* while you sew. However, you do have to *press* while you sew. There is a difference. Pressing is less dragging across the fabric and more, well, pressing, and almost always with steam. The tools for this task are pretty much the same, though. The iron is one item where you may want to be really picky about what you choose.

First and foremost, it has to be a steam iron, and an anti-drip system is a very good feature. You will sometimes want a dry setting too, so be sure your new iron has both options. Auto-off is a must-have feature, although you should always unplug your iron when you are not using it. Your mother said so. Choosing your iron from a fabric store, whether online or actually in the shop, comes highly recommended by this author. Ask questions, too! Most of those sweet folks at the fabric store have years of sewing experience and are more than happy to offer advice on their favorites.

One hundred dollars will likely buy you the best iron you've ever had, but there is quality to be had at even $40 or so. Pressing is the one process, besides your sewing, that has the most impact on the outcome of your sewing project. This cannot be stressed (or pressed) enough!

The Ironing Board

If you're in the market for a new board, you can pay a lot or a little, but do invest based on your enthusiasm for your new hobby, because it should last forever. Go ahead and open it up in the store, if you can, to get a feel for it. Make sure it doesn't wobble, and it's a bonus if it has an adjustable height setting. A nice wide board is really beneficial, especially for ironing quilts and other large items.

If you are battling for floor space, some boards drop down from the wall, out of a cabinet, or from a closet door. Wall-mount hooks are also a good temporary storage option if you want the board out of sight when you are not using it.

An alternative to an ironing board is an ironing blanket or ironing pad. This nifty little portable roll-up or fold-up pad lets you turn a cutting table, countertop, or bed into a usable pressing surface. If you are using an ironing board to press a large item, however, pull the board up next to a large table or bed where your quilt (or whatever your project may be) can spread across it without ending up on the floor.

Other Pressing Matters

These next goodies are not considered *pressing* (as in mandatory); they are *for* pressing.

- A **pressing cloth** is a way to protect your fabric from the effects of the iron as you press during sewing. As long as your heat settings are correct for the particular fabric, pressing the wrong side of the fabric might not be necessary. When you press the right side of the fabric, however, you should use a pressing cloth in order to avoid the heat or pressure from the iron negatively affecting the fabric.

- A **soleplate cover** is another product altogether, but a pretty clever one. It acts like a pressing cloth, but it slips over your iron so that you can easily see what you're working on. It allows you to iron over things like buttons and zippers, and is perfect for pressing delicate fabrics.

- A **pressing ham** is a very firmly packed, contoured, fabric-covered form that looks pretty much like the shape of a whole ham. Over its entire surface, 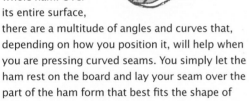 there are a multitude of angles and curves that, depending on how you position it, will help when you are pressing curved seams. You simply let the ham rest on the board and lay your seam over the part of the ham form that best fits the shape of your curved seam, and press.

- A **seam roll** is a long, firmly stuffed cylinder that you can insert underneath long, straight seams and into narrow areas like a sleeve. Having your seam resting on a cylinder-shaped seam roll rather than a flat surface allows you to press only the very center of the seam, right where the fabric is stitched together, and not on the entire seam and seam allowance.

A Cut Above

A good cutting surface at the appropriate height makes all the difference in how accurately your fabric is cut, and whether or not your back is aching at the end of the day. The floor is certainly practical, but it's no fun to sweep before you put your fresh fabrics on the floor. (Sewing is what you do instead of house-cleaning, silly.)

If one item in your cutting-sewing-pressing process had to be located elsewhere, it could be the cutting table. Your first step really should be cutting out all your pieces, anyway. This opens up the possibility to use any table in the house. In fact, the table that eventually becomes your sewing table could first serve as your cutting table.

In general, the height of your cutting table should be about kitchen-counter or kitchen-island height (about 36 inches), and *not* kitchen-table height (about 30 inches). If you are very petite, this height might put your cutting surface too high for reaching all the way across, so do use whichever is more comfortable. If you're teaching your children to sew, just keep a sturdy footstool nearby so they can see what you're working on.

If the size of the tabletop is at least as big as a card table, it's usable. Two card tables pushed together are even better, and pretty economical. Not tall enough? Slide some cinder blocks underneath each leg to raise the height. Bigger is better in the case of the cutting table, but there are some tricks to working on a smaller table. Use a chair or two chairs, side by side, at the end of your table, facing in, to hold your bolt or roll of fabric when you are dealing with a lot of yardage. This way, the bolt or roll of fabric isn't sliding off as you try to cut, and the backs of the chairs are keeping the fabric from landing on the floor.

Sharp Shooters: The Cutting Tools

A cutting tool is another personal thing where one size does not fit all. We each get comfortable with the familiar, or what works for us.

Scissors

You really need only two pairs of scissors: a pair of quality shears for cutting fabrics, and a pair of smaller scissors for snipping threads at the machine, or beside you as you hand-sew. My favorite studio tool by far is my tiny pair of scissors. You should always keep the little ones on a long ribbon around your neck when you're sewing, since they're little and easily misplaced (or is that just me?).

Scissors are definitely another item where quality really does matter. What you spend now will save you later, and with good care and occasional sharpening, they can last you a very long time. In the manufacturing process, scissors are made in one of two ways: they are either forged or stamped. You'll want to get a pair that is forged because they will be much more durable, and of course, they're also pricier. Refer to the concise but practical list below for scissor types and their common uses. This is hardly comprehensive, but for the projects in this book and endless others, it's a good start.

Whatever you choose, take care of your scissors. Dropping them will not only knick your floor and put your feet in danger, but it can also knick the tips of the blades. In some cases, the alignment of the scissors could get knocked out of whack. Save the not-so-good scissors for cutting up things like paper patterns, sequins, plastic, or other non-fabric items in your sewing studio. Reserve your best scissors for the fabrics. If you have two scissors that look alike, tie a small strip of fabric through the sewing scissors' handle as a reminder for yourself and everyone else in the house that they are for fabric only.

Rotary Cutters

The rotary cutter is a different breed of blade altogether. It comes in a large size for all cutting such as your dress patterns and patchwork, or a small size for trimming and smaller craft projects. Using a rotary cutter can give a nice razor-sharp and accurate cut on several layers of fabric with one cut. However, deciding between this and using scissors really just comes down to preference and familiarity. Rotary cutters are not horribly expensive, and, unlike having to keep scissors sharp, you would just replace the disposable blade when it gets dull.

Even if you are comfortable with your scissors, I'd encourage you to give rotary cutting a try. You may find that you like to use scissors for some cutting and a rotary cutter for other cutting. You will probably be amazed at the ease with which it cuts through fabric the first time you use one. They are great if you are doing piece work or are making one pattern several times. I

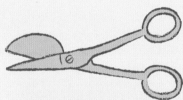

Appliqué scissors or duckbilled scissors have a curved shape on one blade that makes cutting a single layer of fabric easier in appliqué.

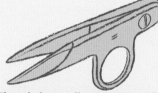

Thread nips or clippers are a small clipper, rather than a standard scissor. They are either spring-loaded or have a hairpin curve of metal as the handle.

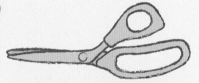

Dressmaking shears are the most common type of scissor used in sewing and are available in 6-inch lengths all the way up to 12-inch lengths—a 7- or 8-inch length is comfortable for most home sewers. Look for shears that have a bent handle, so that the bottom blade will lie flat against your cutting surface.

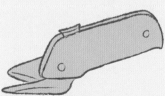

Electric scissors are battery operated. They are a good option for those with hand problems or for someone who needs scissors that are ergonomically designed for comfort.

Embroidery scissors are small, lightweight, and a perfect choice for that petite pair to clip threads as you hand-sew or machine-sew. They are usually only 3 or 4 inches in blade length. Watch the points on these, as they are nice and sharp!

Heavy fabric scissors or tailor's shears are good for cutting through denim, canvas, or multiple layers of fabric. This is where you may want to go with longer blades, like 10 or 12 inches.

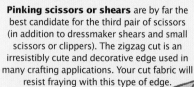

Pinking scissors or shears are by far the best candidate for the third pair of scissors (in addition to dressmaker shears and small scissors or clippers). The zigzag cut is an irresistibly cute and decorative edge used in many crafting applications. Your cut fabric will resist fraying with this type of edge.

Silhouette embroidery scissors or iris scissors are very small and lightweight, with long handles and short, sharp little blades. They are perfect for fine handiwork.

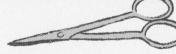

use a rotary cutter for all my quilt cutting and longer cuts on garments, and I save the scissor cutting for inner corners and other picky stuff.

Cutting Mats

Using a rotary cutter most definitely requires the use of a cutting mat. Any other surface would become damaged with rotary cuts, and you would need to toss the blade in the trash almost immediately because it would quickly dull. Most people (including me) prefer to purchase a self-healing cutting mat. This mat is different from the hard mats that you would use with an X-Acto blade.

Getting a mat that is at least 18 x 24 inches is advisable. Anything smaller would have you constantly checking under the fabric to see if you've gone off the mat. Putting two smaller mats together is okay, except that you will undoubtedly always have a few fibers of fabric that didn't get cut because the fabric was pushed into the crease of the two mats when you made the cut. Having one large mat can help you avoid the annoying task of going back to snip those few fibers that you missed.

The bonus of a self-healing cutting mat is its measuring grid, which is so helpful when you are trying to cut a perfect right angle. Believe it or not, though, you should double-check the measurement marks on your mat against a trusty ruler before you rely on them as a definitive guide. In fact, when you are shopping for mats, it wouldn't hurt to have your best ruler on hand to check the measurements for accuracy before you make a purchase. There is sometimes the smallest bit of play in the thick lines of the mat that can get a project, like small-piece quilting, into trouble because the measurements need to be so precise.

Tools for Good Measure

Inching closer toward the goal of a blissful life of sewing, you will find yourself needing to measure things. All kinds of things need to be measured: fabric width and length, arms, legs, busts (yowza!), waists (no!), hips (forget it), hems, seams, windows, dogs, kids, you name it! It all needs to be measured, generally by the yard (¾ yard, ½ yard, ¼ yard), fat quarters (see page 37), inches (⅝ inch, ½ inch, ⅜ inch, ¼ inch), and perhaps centimeters every now and then. Whew! The following is an overview of some tools that you can use for measuring yourself and your environment.

Tape Measure

A tape measure is an essential tool in your beginner kit. I'm not talking about the hefty metal retractable one in the garage toolbox, either. You need the sewing sort, which is a flexible ribbon of either sturdy fabric or plastic with linear units of measure, preferably metric and imperial (inches) measurements on both sides. You'll want to get a good-quality version that doesn't stretch out with a little wear and tear. The basic measuring tape is either 36 inches long (1 yard) or 60 inches long (5 feet). A simple 60-inch tape should meet most of your needs. I like to store mine hanging over a hook (or around my neck) rather than rolled up, to prevent curling.

The tape measure is generally what you use when you are measuring for sewing a garment, or anything else that's not flat. This is precisely why it's flexible.

Yardstick

A yardstick is a yardstick, no matter what anyone says. Wooden, metal, it doesn't matter. Although the metal ones can be prone to bending (i.e., rowdy boys having jousting practice). What they are intended for is measuring anything up to 3 feet, which also just happens to be a yard, or 36 inches.

Sewing Gauge

A sewing gauge is a 6-inch ruler with a sliding marker that you can move to your desired measurement. To hem a skirt all the way around, you would set the sliding part of the sewing gauge at your desired mark and hold the end of the ruler (the 0-inch end) at the bottom edge of the fabric, and turn up the hem at the mark all the way around. It's much quicker this way because you can get a quick visual read of that sliding perpendicular mark, instead of checking the little hairline measurement with every stop around the hem. It's also great for measuring and marking tucks and pleats, and for spacing out buttons and buttonholes. I think of this as my go-to gauge for all small measuring needs that require consistency.

Chapter 2
Details

Small-space dwellers take heart! Most of the items in this chapter only take up square inches and not square feet. Many of the tools discussed here are essential to sewing—such as pins, needles, and thread—while

you may choose to use others for the first time. Like everything put forth in this book, when you purchase a new gadget, always carefully read the instructions first. Practice until you get it right or determine that it's not the tool for you. Don't use it if you can think of a better way on your own. Some of the most ingenious techniques arise out of creative problem solving. Oh, and at the end of the chapter I have some *notions* to share with you too.

Make Your Mark: Marking Tools

Most sewing patterns are printed with all kinds of symbols and markings to illustrate details, like where two pieces should join together or where a pocket, buttonhole, or zipper should be placed. To transfer these symbols onto your fabric, there are several methods of safely marking the fabric, which are like leaving yourself little notes.

To choose the marking tool most suited for your project, you need to consider the type of fabric you are using. If you are going to use a marking tool that can only be removed with water to dissolve and disappear (like a water-soluble pen), then don't use it on fabric that is for dry cleaning only. A tool that makes tiny perforations (like a tracing wheel) is not going to work well on a fabric that has a slick surface (like oil cloth or leather) because the holes or indentations will not go

away. You should always snip a corner of the fabric and test your chosen marking process first, and then see if you can remove it easily. If you can, then you have the green light. If it takes so much rubbing and brushing that you warp or roughen the fabric, that's a red light.

Read through the following descriptions of some available marking tools, and how they can help you make your mark.

Dressmaker's Tracing Paper and Tracing Wheel

This is a combination of tools that you use together to trace lines from a pattern onto fabric without having to move the pattern. The tracing paper is like carbon paper that, when combined with a serrated tracing wheel, will transfer an impression of a dotted line onto fabric. When choosing a tracing paper, choose the lightest one possible that manages to create visible marks on your fabric. You should always try to make your marks on the wrong side of the fabric where possible, unless you are placing a pocket, buttonholes, or zippers.

A bonus use for this tool is to trace an entire pattern onto your fabric, including all the stitching and seams. By just tracing on all the lines, you won't even have to cut out the original pattern pieces to begin with; you can leave them intact for future use of other scaled sizes. Just keep checking underneath your tracing wheel and paper every so often to ensure that you are making the line dark enough to see.

Tailor's Chalk

Tailor's chalk is a very traditional little marker that you can remove quite easily and that will work well on almost any type of fabric. Use a version of this product that has a chalk base and not a wax base, because it will be less likely to leave any residue. There are often different colors to choose from that will make your marks show up on a variety of colored fabrics.

Fabric-Marking Pens

Fabric-marking pens are a more modern version of tailor's chalk. These pens are available in both air-soluble and wash-away (or water-soluble) versions. The non-permanent pens are excellent for marking areas for embellishment or embroidery. You should not use an iron on these marks; you should let them dissolve or wash them away first.

Alternatives to Marking Tools

You don't have to purchase marking tools from a fabric store. You can use little sticker dots from an office supply store for marking snaps, buttons, or the corners of a pocket location. Draw the exact placement of the item with a pen mark on the sticker to avoid marking on the fabric at all.

Soap-y

You can also use a small sliver of soap when it becomes too small to use for its intended purposes. Watch out for soap that is made with scented oils or a lot of additives because they will most likely leave a residue on your fabric. It's best to go with a very simple soap like Ivory.

Snip-y and Stitch-y

And finally, good old-fashioned clipping, snipping, notching, and just plain hand stitching are wonderful means to leave breadcrumb clues on the path to completing the finer details of a project (see pages 40 and 41 in Chapter 4).

On Pins and Needles
Pinning It Down

Pins are the sharp little friends that keep pattern pieces together and hold tucks, pleats, and hems in place as you make your way from the cutting table to the sewing machine. They can also act as a fantastic marking tool. If you need to know where to stop a dart, where a collar should be joined, or how long a pleat should be stitched, then sticking a pin in the fabric is a perfect option for marking your start and stop points as directed by your pattern. Inserting pins perpendicular to each other can illustrate a corner for perfect pocket placement (say that ten times fast). If you have very fine or delicate fabric, you may not want to use pins for marking, however, because the holes may not go away. It is, of course, advisable to still use them to hold a seam in place, even with delicate fabric, before and during machine stitching. In this case, just be sure to poke them only through the part of the fabric that will become the seam allowance, which won't be visible once you finish the item.

You should choose quality pins for your sewing, which means, at the very least, that they need to be rust proof. Pins come with plain heads, plastic heads, glass heads, and all kinds of fancy decorative heads, as well. Large round heads or decorative heads are great because they are easy to pick up. Colorful heads make pins easy to spot on the floor before you spot them in your foot. Glass head pins are very useful because they won't melt when under or very near the iron.

Note: Ideally, you shouldn't be running over your pinned fabric with an iron anyway, because this can set a pin mark into your fabric. It will also scratch your iron.

You can buy magnetic pins, but the main problem with them is that they are magnetic. I am not a fan. Seriously. They stick to each other, and other metal things, which is not especially helpful. There are special pleating pins that are shorter and very fine, which are well suited for delicate fabrics. The shortest pins offered would be appliqué or sequin pins. If you are quilting, then long and very thin, straight pins are best; they glide right in and out of the fabric with ease, and seldom leave a mark. If you want a decorative head on your quilting pins, then choose those with flat silhouette shapes that will lie flat against your quilting surface. There are also T-head pins, which are just that—T-headed, and can be used for almost anything a regular straight pin is used for. While you want the sharpest points available, reserve a set of ballpoint pins to be used with knits, which won't catch on the threads of the fabric. If you do not want pin marks in your fabric, then use metal clips—yup, just like the plain hair clips—and save one for your bangs.

Safety pins are very handy to have around, and you would want to use the non-corrosive kind, in a small size like No.1 or the 1-inch length. Savvy quilters also use them to hold together multiple layers of fabric for machine quilting; curved safety pins are especially good to pin through thick layers of fabric and batting. When working on a multi-pieced appliqué, use safety pins instead of straight pins so you won't lose any. Really large safety pins are also nice for sticking in the end of elastic to help you thread it through a waistband. There are fancier tools for that, with fancier names, but a fat safety pin will do the job on short runs. Overall, just be sure that any safety pins you purchase are made to use on fabric.

Needles in Your Play Stack

By now, you must realize that almost every tool and supply category for sewing comes with a long list of varieties. There is a needle made specifically for every different type of situation. The general two categories of needles are hand-sewing needles and machine-sewing needles.

Hand-Sewing Needles

Hand-sewing needles come in 10 different sizes, from No.1 through No.10. The needles at the No.1 end are thicker and are for very coarse fabrics. On the other end, the No.10 needle is very fine and is, in turn, made for finer, more delicate materials. In addition to the numbered system, there are common types of needles; here is a concise list of them:

- **Appliqué needles** are short, very fine needles for hand appliqué or small, detailed work on delicate fabrics.
- **Beading needles** are very fine and long needles, perfect for stringing beads or doing bead embellishment on fabric.
- **Quilting needles or betweens** are very short and fine needles with round eyes, allowing the quilter to make quick stitches in a sort of rocking motion.
- **Chenille needles** are one of the larger needles, with large eyes and very sharp points. They are made for doing ribbon embroidery and crewel, and for tying quilts with thicker threads.
- **Clover needles or leather needles** have a unique triangular point that can pierce leather without tearing it.

- **Cotton Darners** are very long with sharp points, and are ideal for mending, basting (long stitches), and darning. They are perfect for mending any type of cotton or wool. Similar to this category are *Milliners,* which are used in hat making.
- **Easy thread needles or Calyx-eyed sharps** actually have a little slot in the top of the eye, which means that you don't thread them, you slot them. These are pretty handy, indeed, especially if you have difficulty threading a standard needle.
- **Embroidery needles** are similar to chenille needles and sharps, but they usually have an eye that's longer and narrower. They are good for general hand-sewing.
- **Sharps** are to needles as shears are to scissors; they are your typical all-purpose needles, essential in your beginner's kit. The sizes you would want to have on hand are between 7 and 9, which are suitable for most light- to medium-weight fabrics.
- **Yarn Darners** are the heaviest needles, with large eyes, and they are used for stitching and darning with yarn. A tapestry needle would be very similar to this.

With only a few of these basic needles, you'll be able to do the hand sewing required for the projects in this book, like blind stitching and other clever tricks that I discuss in Chapter 5.

Machine-Sewing Needles

Assuming you own a sewing machine or are using someone else's, you'll need to replace the needles at some point. A new needle should give you 6 to 10 hours of solid sewing time before you need to replace it, as it will become dull if you haven't already broken it first (join the club).

All machine-sewing needles generally look the same, but they are not. The correct needle really does make a huge difference in the quality of your stitches. Using the wrong needle can put your machine's timing out of whack, ruin or break your thread, or wreck your seams. Choosing the correct needle is not difficult; it's just imperative.

The first place that you should look to find which needle to buy is in your sewing machine's manual. Almost every home sewing machine uses the 130/705H needle system. This just means that it will use the standard sizes and types of machine needles that are easily found at a fabric store.

Needles are available in a variety of sizes and types: The size tells you how big the needle is, and the type refers to the kind of needle point. Different types of fabrics will require different sizes and needle points to prevent damage or big holes in the fabric as you stitch.

Needling by the Numbers

Just like when buying fancy clothes, you are usually confronted with both the European and American sizing systems. Americans use needles from size 8 to size 19—the smaller numbers are the smaller needles, and the larger numbers are the larger needles. The numbers don't mean anything special; it's just an arbitrary system. The extravagant and ever-particular Europeans, however, use a number system that refers to the actual diameter of the shaft above the eye of the needle. You only need to be aware of the European size because it will often be paired with the American size, such as 60/8 for a size-8 needle, or 70/10 for a size-10 needle. Get it? Don't get it? Then refer to the chart below.

Oh, Good Point

So you've figured out the weight of the fabric and the size of the needle that you need. Now you need to consider the type of the fabric to determine the type of the point your needle should have. There are around a dozen or so basic types of needles for a sewing machine. Why could this possibly matter? Well, the new sewer may not see the difference in stitch quality between using a 60/8 Universal point and a 60/8 Sharp point, but the more experience you have, the pickier you may become. Some machine-needle manufacturers will color-code the needle with a band of color, so that you will know which type you have sticking in your pin cushion. For basic machine stitching, here is a rundown of needle types:

- **Universal point needles** will do almost all of your tricks. The name says it all.
- **Ballpoint needles** are designed with a more rounded tip so that they won't catch on knit or stretchy fabrics.
- **Stretch needles** are great if you have really stretchy fabrics with spandex, or if they're highly elasticized.
- **Embroidery needles** have a larger eye, are a little more rounded on the tip, and have a deep scarf (or groove) for the thicker decorative threads to nestle into as they are driven into your gorgeous embroidery work.

Needle Size Conversion Chart

European	American	Fabric Weight	Fabric Examples
60	8	light	very sheer fabric
65	9	light	lightweight, see–through fabric
70	10	light–medium	light T–shirt fabric
75	11	medium	blouse fabric
80	12	medium–heavy	lightweight denim
90	14	heavy	corduroy, suiting
100	16	heavy	medium–weight denim
110	18	very heavy	jeans
120	19	very heavy	canvas

Note: If you are having trouble choosing the right needle, your helpful sewing shop should be able to guide you once you've shared your project and fabric choice with them.

- **Sharp point needles or Microtext needles** are for extra-fine fabrics. They do very well on a high thread-count cotton or for machine-piecing a quilt. The smallest of these needles is the 60/8 size, and they work well with really tiny and fine threads.
- **Quilting needles** have a tapered point and are generally stronger, which makes them suitable for stitching through multiple layers of fabrics and over junctures where many seams come together.
- **Metallica thread needles** are the rock stars of the needles. They are coated in Teflon (go figure, not spandex?) to allow metallic threads to slip through with less friction. You would also use these needles when sewing with monofilament or invisible threads.
- **Topstitching needles** have an extra-large eye and deeper scarf to hold the heavyweight topstitching threads in place for smooth topstitching.

You'll most likely know when the needle is dull if you pay attention to the kinds of holes it leaves in the fabric, or if the machine is making an extra kind of *bump* sound as the needle enters the fabric. A dull needle will also leave your stitch quality less than perfect. Changing the needle is one of the main troubleshooting solutions when you are experiencing stitch-quality issues with your machine. Do keep plenty on hand, because if you are new to the sewing machine, you will likely break some. Actually, you'll do that anyway. It is not fun to have to quit your sewing when you run out of needles and the fabric store is closed. That always makes me cry.

If this has completely bored you to tears or thoroughly confused you, just buy a whole bunch of size-12 needles, and you could sew happily for a good long time.

Cozy Cushions, a Place to Call Home

Can you give a hardworking pin or needle a home? Sure you can! There are so many darling little collectible pin cushions to be had these days. The ever-classic and familiar red tomato cushion with the emery-filled strawberry is never a wrong choice, and wristband pin cushions are also very handy.

I always find that keeping my pins in a big pin cushion is so much easier than digging them out of a box. I also like the cushion to be especially bulky, so that I can poke using only my peripheral vision as I stitch away. Keep your sewing machine needles in their case until they've been used, but always store your non-throw-away machine needles in a pin cushion once you've switched them out. Making a pin cushion is a fabulous first sewing project, so try the "Pin Cushion Caddy" project in Chapter 6. It's a pin cushion and so much more!

Use Your Thread

In general, you should choose thread to be compatible with the fabric's structure and fiber content. A cotton thread wouldn't be suitable for a synthetic fabric because the cotton thread could shrink up when laundered, causing the synthetic, which won't shrink, to pucker up at the stitch lines. Additionally, you should choose thread based on what type of sewing you will be doing, whether it's general sewing like the projects in this book, or specialty sewing like machine embroidery or quilting. In the following list, I'm sticking to the standard machine-sewing threads, which will also work for general hand sewing.

- **Cotton thread** in a medium thickness, such as size 50, is perfect for light- or medium-weight cottons, rayons, and linens. Because it doesn't really stretch or give at all, it isn't recommended for knits. Mercerized cotton is best because it's been finished to be smooth and luminous. This also helps the range of colors that it comes in to be rich and saturated.
- **Polyester thread** in the same size as cotton thread (50) is another all-purpose thread, and is good for woven synthetics or knit (stretchy) synthetics. It usually has a waxy coating that helps it easily glide through the fabrics for smooth stitching.

- **Cotton-wrapped polyester thread** is just what you would expect: a combination thread that is suited for combination materials such as blends.

- **Silk thread** is very fine, versatile, and strong. It is recommended for sewing on both silk and wool, and it is used a lot in tailoring because of its elasticity.

- **Nylon thread** is a strong and fine thread used for sewing light- to medium-weight synthetic fabrics, such as nylon tricot.

- **Heavy-duty threads** are available in cotton, polyester, and cotton-wrapped polyester varieties. They are coarse, usually size 40, and are recommended for heavy-duty sewing with canvas, denim, or upholstery fabrics.

If you have two colors of thread that are both close to the fabric color but neither is perfect, it's a good rule of thumb to go with the darker of the two. When sewing with printed fabrics or over multiple-pieced fabrics, I usually choose the color that is most dominant, or the background color. Or you could choose a thread color to be purposefully in contrast to the fabric.

Don't buy cheap thread; it is prone to splitting and breaking in the machine and when hand sewing. Good thread should have well-dyed, even color (unless you want the funky variegated ones), and be smooth and luminous. Also, when removing thread from your machine, cut it up top near the spool and pull the remaining strand downward and out from the needle shaft. Just pulling the thread up and out from the top of the machine will leave an unwanted build-up of thread fiber inside the machine.

Mystery Tools

The following is a list of some items that are considered must-haves by some, and hardly worth the bother by others.

- A **seam ripper** should be at the top of the list. You will inevitably undo what you've sewn, and so this is an indispensable tool. It's also ideal for slitting buttonholes that you've sewn on the machine.

- **Bamboo point turners** are very simple little helpers that you can add to your stash for a few dollars. They're pointed on one end for gently poking out points like collars, and curved on the other end for inserting between layers of curved seams to smooth them out. Bamboo is a soft wood that won't hurt your fabric, and it is not so sharp that it will poke through your sewn corner like a pair of scissors would.

- **Loop turners** are used to turn a long, narrow tube of sewn fabric right side out after stitching. Again, they're inexpensive and very basic. It's ideal for spaghetti straps, purse straps, drawstrings, or button loops.

- **Bodkins** are used for threading elastic, ribbon, or drawstrings through casings, if you don't fancy using the large safety pin trick.

- A **needle threader** is a cute little thing, and you'll never guess what it does.

- **Thimbles** are a very classic and helpful sewing must-have, especially if you like to appliqué, quilt, or do other handiwork. They protect your finger as you press the needle repeatedly through the fabric. Which finger you use depends on your particular style of sewing.

- **Beeswax** is sometimes used to run threads across to increase their strength before sewing with them.

Half the fun in making your sewing sanctuary a cozy one is in how you choose to tuck away, organize, or display your tools and supplies. A rainbow of threads on a thread rack is an inviting spread of eye-candy. Rows of tins, bins, and baskets can smartly hold all your gadgets on a brightly colored bookshelf. You can reference magazines and design stores for storage ideas, or repurpose old or vintage items you love; these are both great ways to come up with clever organizational solutions.

Notion Nation

Almost every single store that sells fabric and sewing-related items has a different idea about what falls under the category of *notions*. That fact will not hinder you from acquiring what you need for your sewing projects. In the broadest definition of the term, a notion is any tool, material, substance, trim, detail, or accessory that you employ in your sewing that is not the fabric or the sewing machine. I've discussed everything from pins and needles to bodkins, so far. All these gadgets and tools would sometimes fall into the notions category, either at an online store or a brick-and-mortar store. Even thread and marking tools could be considered notions.

I think of notions in a more narrow definition, which would be any item or material, other than fabric, that becomes part of the finished product, even if it's something that is not visible in the end, like an interfacing or a spray-on fabric stiffener. Because this book employs this definition of a notion, all the previously discussed items would be considered tools.

Most stores where you buy fabric should also carry all your basic notions, but to a varying degree. If your favorite place to buy fabric is a quilt shop, then they will have notions that cater to the needs of a typical quilter. A home décor textile shop will be more likely to have notions and accessories that have more to do with curtains, couches, and comforters, but have no ribbons, buttons, or laces. And while the larger-chain fabric stores will have practically every gadget and notion available to humankind, the locally owned boutique-style fabric store will be more likely to carry the most impressive collection of imported laces and ribbons.

Because there are so many different types of notions, having an overview of the categories, common items within those categories, and common uses is helpful. Refer to the following section for a general reference of notions as defined by this book, which doesn't include items that I've put in the tool category. This is just an overview, and I encourage you to spend a day in your favorite store exploring all the oddities within.

Closures

When finding closure, you'll find those items that you would use to close a garment, or some other item like a couch cushion or a pillow sham. Buttons, clasps, snaps, hooks, zippers, Velcro, and variations on all these items are part of this category. There are thousands of types that suit all purposes, either decorative or functional.

The uses for these items are quite self-explanatory, but skip over to "Zippity Hoorah: The Centered Zipper" in Chapter 4 and "Hole-y Buttons" in Chapter 5 for tips on sewing with some of them.

Elastic

There are so many ways to stretch your sewing with elastics. Elastic comes in many different widths and is either sold by the yard or prepackaged in different lengths. Some elastic is suited for the waistband of a skirt, while thinner cord-like varieties are intended solely for beading a stretchy bracelet. Metallic elastic cording would also be in this section of the store, although you'll likely use that to wrap a present.

Interfacing and Stabilizers

Just face it, interfacing and stabilizers are items that help give body or crispness to fabric, often for use in sewing garments. If you're making a cotton blouse, you may want to leave the fabric soft and supple in the torso, but give the collar more body or stiffness with interfacing. Other places you may use interfacing in a garment are along the button placket (the shirt edge that has the row of buttonholes), in a waistband, or in a very structured jacket. In general, interfacing makes a fabric either stiffer or thicker, or helps it to retain shape. Also, if you embellish a fabric with machine or handstitching, you would want to stabilize a thinner fabric from behind to prevent tearing and stretching.

Most interfacings are either pressed onto the wrong side of the fabric with an iron, or sewn on by machine. Beyond the material interfacings, which are sold by the yard or in a package, there are also treatments for fabric that come in the form of a spray or liquid. Different still would be a tear-away interfacing that you only use during the task at hand, like appliqué or sewing a buttonhole. You would then tear away all the leftover interfacing that isn't sewn into place by whatever technique you've used. This is useful when you are using sheer fabrics and don't want to see the interfacing through the material.

As previously mentioned, some of the interfacings you'll use are pressed in with an iron and are known as *fusibles*. A fusible can have a variety of thicknesses, from extremely thin and sheer to thick and almost cardboard-like. It's often referred to as fusible *web,* and it's a synthetic material with a surface that will melt when heated. A thinner variety with a paper backing on both sides could be used just for its adhesive qualities to fuse two fabrics together, or to fuse fabric to wood or many other surfaces. It also comes in tape form to create no-sew seams or to serve as a quick fix when you have an unraveled hemline. The very heavy-duty fusibles are used for their structural qualities and can turn fabric into sculpture very quickly. (See the "Cozy Cubes" project and "Pin Cushion Caddy" project in Chapter 6.) The most important thing to remember about all interfacings and fusibles is to follow the manufacturer's instructions. The adhesive used in many fusible products is so strong that it may gum up your needle if you use the machine to sew through it, so beware. All of them are different and require different techniques, heat settings, and *practice.*

Hardware

Sewing isn't always soft and sweet. There is a little grit thrown in now and then with the use of hardware. Things like buckles, D-rings, purse handles, swivel hooks, and grommets can all be found in the notions section of a fabric store. You'll use grommets, also called *eyelets,* for the "Wall Pockets" project in Chapter 6.

Fillers

Pillow forms, foam, stuffing, and quilt batting all play a very important (and very cozy) part in many projects for the home. Where would teddy bears be without their stuffing? How would a quilt keep you warm in the winter without the dense fiber layered between the fabrics? Keep reading to learn how to properly stuff your project.

Pillow Forms

When making a pillow or a cushion, there are many options of what to fill it with. The most obvious, and perhaps the easiest, is a pre-made, fabric-covered, filled form that is ready to go. These come in a myriad of sizes and have various fiber contents from cotton to down feathers. So if you have allergies, you should pay attention to the content listing.

Foam

When making something generally rectangular and flat, like a seat cushion, it's sometimes best to use foam because of its regular thickness. You can buy foam either pre-cut and packaged in standard chair-cushion sizes, or sold by the yard (or inches) in various thicknesses. Not only will the dimension and thickness vary, but so will the density of the foam. You wouldn't want really squishy foam for a couch cushion, but a comfortably dense one, instead—unless, of course, you like getting lost in your couch.

Stuffing

Sometimes called *fiberfill,* this loose, cotton-like fiber is ideal for making pin cushions, soft crafts, toys, and other cushy items. Because it breaks apart and requires you to manually stuff your sewn items, you can form it into any shape that you desire, even a skinny, polka-dotted monkey. The outcome of your skinny, polka-dotted monkey will also vary, depending on how loosely or densely you stuff it. Inconsistency and lumps usually happen when you are pushing in handfuls of fiber that are too large.

Batting

Batting is the soft, stuffing-like layer that goes between a quilt top (the decorative or top side) and the backing. It's usually sold in various standard sizes and is rolled up in a package like a sleeping bag. There are a wide variety of quilt battings available that are made up of various fiber contents. Cotton battings are warm and natural, like you might expect. Polyester battings are durable but maybe not as comfortable to sleep under, because they don't breathe well. A polyester/cotton blend would be a very usable combination and is easier to perform the quilt stitches on because it's less dense. Wool batting is especially warm and dense.

The term *loft* refers to the thickness and resilience of the batting. High loft would be fluffier and suitable for minimal quilt stitches or tied quilts. Medium loft is still nice and puffy, but has a reasonable amount of loft that can work easily underneath a machine-quilting process. Low loft would be more like an old-fashioned quilt that is thinner, softer, and less stiff. All quilts will soften over time.

Nice and Trim

There are many, many categories of trim, and within each, there are thousands of options. If you compare fabric shopping to clothing shopping, I think of the trims like jewelry or shoes. Sometimes it just takes finding that perfect trim to inspire an entire project or collection of items. There are also less-expected combinations of trims and notions that can make cute and quirky one-of-a-kind items, which you could use for projects like the "Doodad Pillow" in Chapter 8. Below is a list of common trim categories.

Ribbons and Lace

The ribbon category ranges from very wide, decorative ribbon that is embellished to be a work of art, to a simple, skinny, smooth satin ribbon in a rainbow of colors. There are also several printed varieties in every pattern under the sun. There are sheer ribbons, thick grosgrain ribbons, satin ribbons, and, really, the same textures you might find in fabric.

There are too many uses for ribbon to name them all, but some less obvious ones include as spaghetti straps, applied elastic, or drawstring casings; sculptural ribbon embellishment; ruffling into a trim; and striping an otherwise solid fabric.

Fringes

Fringes can be anything from heavy, dangling beads to light and fluffy ostrich feathers. A fringe is usually made up of two parts: a flatter top part (sometimes called a *lip* or *header*) that is either designed to be shown or to be hidden in a seam, and the lower decorative part, which either dangles or is designed to peek out from a hemline or from in between seams.

Cording and Piping

Non-decorative cording is the material you would buy to create what's known as *piping*. The uncovered cording material looks like a spool of chunky, lightweight rope that varies from fat and puffy to thin and rope-like. Decorative piping is created by wrapping lengths of fabric, cut on the grain or on the bias, around the cording to create a custom trim. Refer to "Pipe Dream" in Chapter 4 for tips on sewing with this type of trim, as well as making your own.

Rickrack

This common and colorful trim has zigged and zagged throughout home-sewn history. It has never truly gone out of style, which is likely why it's often given its own spot in sewing stores apart from the trims. The most common type of rickrack is sold prepackaged in various widths and in a rainbow of colors, even rainbow-colored. It is also sold by the yard, sometimes in a variety of sizes, and even with a velvety texture. Rickrack is as adorable sewn on top of a garment or an accessory as it is sewn on the underside of a sleeve cuff or dress hem, with just half of it peeking out from the bottom for a scalloped effect.

Seam Binding or Bias Tape

Usually prepackaged, seam binding and hem tapes come in a wide variety of colors and help blend the double thickness of a hem with the single thickness of the garment so that ridges or bumps don't show through on the outside. They also help to cover the raw edges from your garment's bottom edge to prevent fraying. Sometimes these are also called *hem facings* and can be made from either a lining-type material or a lace.

While you can use binding for decorative purposes, it's typically used for finishing off the edges of something. A final step in quilting is to bind the quilt so that the edges are finished and have a sort of narrow frame around them. This is best done with strips of fabric cut on the bias or with prepackaged bias tapes, which serve the same purpose. Bias tape is usually either single-, double-folded, or triple-folded and creased so that you can wrap it around a fabric edge, sandwiching the unfinished edges inside for a nice finish. Some of the triple-folded varieties have their outer creases set at two different widths to guide your stitch lines, so that when making the second and final stitch, the underside will be caught in the same seam. Bindings cut on the grain would not be especially flexible and therefore would not bind curved items very well. See "Maybe I'm Bias" in Chapter 4 for tips on cutting your own bias strips.

Chapter 3
Let's Bolt

Perhaps the greatest opportunity to exercise your creativity and personal aesthetic in any sewing project is with the fabrics that you choose. Very often your final result has so much more to do with the look of your fabric than it does with the degree of

difficulty in the pattern you've used. The varieties in weight, color, combinations, print, fiber content, look, and feel are absolutely endless. While 100-percent cottons are my favorite type of fabric to sew with, they are also the best for beginners. They are so easy to cut, sew, press, and care for; it's hard to ignore them. It's also hard to not fall in love with the variety of prints and colors. All of those gorgeous cottons seem like characters in a narrative that tells the story of how important sewing is becoming. Again. More and more people are gaining a new appreciation for making their own items for their home, for themselves, and for gifts. Fabric companies have happily responded by seeking out designers in all genres to design beautiful and expressive fabric collections that pack the miles of aisles that we all love to stroll. This chapter offers a little knowledge in textiles, some color theory, and also helps with identifying what you're looking for, where to find it, and how to take care of all that fabric. Also, you'll make sense of all those words the folks at the cutting counter throw around so easily when you're trying to buy fabric.

Naming Names

When identifying different fabrics, there are as many names that refer to the look and design of a given fabric as there are names that refer to the fiber content. Sometimes you will see both the terms combined. For instance, *cotton gingham* describes both the fiber content and the style of the weave or design of

the fabric. What this doesn't tell you, though, is the weight of the fabric. Most cotton ginghams are light to medium-weight, while others are very light and virtually sheer. However, if a fabric is just called *gingham,* you wouldn't know whether it is cotton, rayon, polyester, or a combination of all three fibers. There are so many blends out there that are comprised of both natural and synthetic materials that you couldn't use one word to describe them if you tried. Of course, you could just say *blend.* But blended what? To properly care for the item you'll be making, it is imperative to know the fiber content. Just when you have familiarized yourself with the typical fiber content of a given fabric, you'll find that broadcloth isn't always cotton and brocade isn't always silk. There will always be variations on the traditional.

Don't let the complexities of fabric names and textile terms intimidate you. As most of us prance into the fabric store, we will first respond to the choices in terms of their color and design. When you are purchasing fabric just to grow your stash and with nothing specific in mind, it will matter less what type of fabric it is. You may decide only after you've bought it what to do with it. Join the club. The name of the fabric will not likely make a difference to you as long as it looks and feels the way you want it to. However, if you have a little knowledge of the different types of fabrics and their names, it will help you determine whether or not that gorgeous celadon/butter-cream/melon-pink floral print that you can't live without is more suitable as a skirt or as a slipcover. Or just maybe it would be perfect for both.

Wovens versus Knits

Speaking very generally, fabrics perform in one of two ways: they either stretch or they don't. Most call these two categories either *woven* fabrics, which don't stretch, or *knit* fabrics, which do stretch. Traditionally, quilting-weight cottons, broadcloths, denim, canvas, corduroy, and so forth are woven materials and don't really have any *give* to them, meaning they don't stretch. Cloth is woven by a process that employs vertical threads called *warp* threads, and horizontal threads called *weft* threads. These threads are woven very tightly at a 90-degree angle to each other so that when you tug on them, either lengthwise or crosswise, they don't stretch. It would be like tugging on a length of your sewing thread. (They do stretch, however, if tugged at an angle or on the *bias,* which I'll cover in the section, "Tedious Terms," later in this chapter.)

Knit fabrics have loops of fiber, which allow the fabric to stretch just like a sweater that has been knit. Most knit fabrics are machine-made, and there are tons of different types of knits with varying degrees of stretch. They might stretch in only one direction or in all directions. Whether or not a fabric stretches is one of the most important considerations when you are sewing from a specific pattern. If the pattern calls for a stretch material, you have to use a stretch material. If it calls for woven material, it wouldn't hurt for the fabric to have a little stretch, especially if it is a woven material with just a small percentage of lycra, or spandex, in it. When you are sewing with it, though, the fabric will behave differently than a regular woven. It'll stretch. Go figure.

If you are sewing specifically from a pattern that you've purchased (or are about to purchase), don't forget to look at the back of the envelope or perhaps on the inner instruction sheet for guidelines on types of fabric to choose.

Frolic in the Fabric

Where to start? Will it be the local, large, fabric store chain? Or what about that little quilt shop? Is it possible to find quality fabrics online? How will you know if the fabric is the right color or if you'll like the feel of it if you can't touch it first? These are all questions that may take some time and experience to answer for yourself. Read on for a little insight on purchasing fabric.

Ch-ch-chain

As I stated at the beginning of this chapter, there is a greater demand for well-designed fabric now than ever. In the larger fabric and craft-store chains, there are definitely some quality fabrics to be had, and they are a good place to start. There are often monthly specials, coupons, and sales to take advantage of, especially if you join the mailing list of your local store. You can get some serious deals if you plan your projects around the types of sales that are happening. The larger chains are also good places to get the things that you go through quickly, like thread, hand needles, machine needles, zippers, and other notions.

Locals, Locals, Locals

Independent retailers that are not part of a national chain frequently carry lines of fabric by textile designers and companies that are not sold at chain stores. By the same token, because the independent stores are not buying in the same large bulk as the chains, they often cannot offer the same kind of price breaks on fabric. While you may end up paying a little more, it's likely that the service and relationship you can build in a smaller setting is what makes it worth coming back. Often retailers will offer to special-order something for you as long as you are buying in a large enough quantity.

Type, Click, Cut, and Stitch

Like everything else, if you don't want to (or can't) leave your house, it won't stop you from buying fabric. You can find anything online that you can find in a brick-and-mortar store. The only drawback would be not being able to get a real-life color read on the fabrics or a sense of how they feel. If you familiarize yourself with the general quality of a fabric company and can seek out their products online, you'll have more confidence as you order. Some online stores are better than others about the visuals on their sites, and they offer very accurate photography of their fabric selections. Even so, we are all looking at the virtual world through different monitors, and so there will be differences in accuracy.

Online fabric shops will often let you have a sample cut of something first before you buy your larger quantity. While you are asking about that, go ahead and find out about the return policy to be sure it's easy to go through if your order ends up not being what you were looking for. Always get the return policy in writing, and not just verbally over the phone. Hopefully, any online shop that you frequent with your fingers will have the policy posted on an information or FAQ page. There are bunches of fabulous fabric finds out there that are just a click away.

Thrifting for Threads

There's vintage and then there's *vintage.* A lot of what we see in the fabric stores these days is inspired by vintage textiles of various decades. There are also fabrics that are more than inspired by vintage; they are the actual vintage prints that have either been reprinted in a new color palette or reproduced in their original glory. There is what's called a vintage *document,* which is a print that no longer has a copyright or perhaps never had one to begin with. Fabric designers and companies will often buy up the rights to these documents and have them reprinted, sometimes manipulating the forms, combining them with modern elements, or just changing the colors a bit. So if you decide to thrift for your threads, you may be surprised to find some of your favorite designer goods among the piles of fabric at an estate sale, yard sale, thrift store, or flea market.

Collecting old textiles that are either still in their original state on a bolt, or already made into something like curtains, is a great way to enhance your collection. Be sure that the fabric still feels durable and is free from stain and moth damage. Your dry cleaner, or local fabric store may be able to help you determine the general content of a found fabric so that you can care for it properly. A good washing or dry cleaning can rid an old textile of its musty odor. You can repurpose many shower curtains, table linens, bedspreads, and even old clothing into new items for yourself. So don't just buy the inspired fabrics; treat yourself and seek out the authentic oldies, too. Half the fun is in the hunt, after all.

Repeating Yourself: How to Choose Prints and Colors

I could fill all the pages of this book with just information for exploring and understanding what works well when choosing printed fabric designs for your sewing projects. It is possibly one of the hardest things for many new sewers, and the choices are only getting more abundant.

I've already compared buying clothes to buying fabric because many of the same rules apply, especially if you are garment sewing. How many times have you chosen a solid-colored blouse for fear of growing tired of the printed one? Or maybe you are on the opposite end of the spectrum and have a fear of solids. Whatever the case, you know what you like, so trust yourself.

The approach that you take in choosing fabrics will vary, depending on whether you are making a craft, a home accessory, or a garment, for yourself or someone else. If you are making a garment with a single fabric, then shop for the fabric just like you would shop for a garment. You would want the colors to look good on whoever will be wearing it, or perhaps you'll be matching it to a favorite sweater. If you are making something from a mix of more than one fabric, you'll want to put a little more thought into it. There is an art form to mixing patterns and prints together, and also to combining colors effectively. There's also an art form to completely disregarding the rules and going for it (think crazy quilts). If the *no-rules* approach is your aesthetic, congratulations, you are a brave soul. If you'd like some rules, however, I'll give you a few.

Colder, Cold, Warm, Warmer, Hot

Color is what most people respond to first, and so you can always start there when choosing your fabrics. Color theory is a vibrant science and a really intriguing one. It's great to familiarize yourself with the flow of the spectrum and perhaps get your hands on a color chart or a color wheel. You should be able to find one of these at a craft store or any art and design supply store. The color wheel is a wonderful tool that will help you understand which colors harmonize and which colors stand out against each other. On the following page, I've created a color wheel using various fabric swatches.

Speaking very generally, there are two main color families, often referred to as warm colors and cool colors. The warm colors are the reds, oranges, yellows, pinks, rusts, and rich browns (think sunset and warmth). The cool colors are the blues, greens, purples, and teals (think water and coolness). Each of the colors in these families blends from one into the next around the color wheel. So any colors that are next to each other on the wheel would be harmonious and considered to be in the same color family. The greens and the violets are like the connectors between warm and cool colors that could go either way, depending on their hue. The wheel itself is very useful in finding opposite colors that will pop against each other and cause visual tension. The opposite of any color is also called its *complement,* and can be found by looking directly across the color wheel from your chosen color. For example, if you choose an orange palette, the accent color would be blue because blue is the complement, or opposite, of orange.

Neutral colors like white, creams, tans, grays, and even variations of black will usually fall into a cool or warm category, depending on the particular hue of the neutral. For instance, you can compare two different black fabrics side by side, and one will be more blue-black and the other more brown-black. There are indeed neutrals that are truly neutral, as in neither warm nor cool. The more neutrals you use in an overall scheme, the quieter, softer, and more naturalistic the look will be.

Cooking with Color

I like to think of combining colors like recipes. Three of the different ways to combine colors are by using a completely monochromatic (one-color) scheme, a generally monochromatic scheme with an accent, and a fully multicolored scheme. Within each of these three schemes, there are variations you can play with based on saturation (how rich the color is), and different print styles that will change the overall feel of your result. The following paragraphs and photographs help to illustrate these three basic color recipes, and I hope they will inspire some yummy sewing ideas.

Color Recipe One: Monochromatic

If you are choosing to work with a singular color scheme when combining your fabrics, choose a warm range or a cool range of fabrics. An example of this would be choosing all shades of reds, pinks, oranges, and yellows in various prints and motifs.

As shown above (and also on this book's cover), I used very deep and saturated warm tones as well as some medium intensity tones for a vibrant all over feel. When choosing just warm tones, the focus becomes the shapes in the fabric designs, and the variety comes from the various depths of color.

Different still would be to choose only one main color to work with, such as red. Rather than looking for subtleties in shade to combine as above, you would look for differences in scale, choosing large, red prints, along with tiny prints, checks, and dots. Then, all of a sudden, you would be playing more with form than with color. Yet you would have made such a colorful statement!

Color Recipe Two: Monochromatic with an Accent

This option would be achieved by choosing mostly one color or one range (either cool or warm) to work with, and then using an accent color to add a visual pop. This is a very fun trick, especially if you are patch-working fabrics together. If you choose a pale-green palette, the ideal accent color would be red or pink (see below). Using an accent color in any situation is like putting black and white together; it creates visual tension and interest.

If you want to get even more focused, you could choose just two warm colors, like pink and yellow, and only choose very small and pale prints, as shown in the above selection. The result would be very delicate and airy. Either of these two choices would be a monochromatic scheme but would have a drastically different outcome.

The effect is similar if you choose an all-neutral palette and combine it with an accent of bold color, or a single fabric with an accent of a striking print (see below). The accent itself can appear in the form of a trim around a skirt, straps at the top of a blouse, the binding on a quilt, or the lining of a handbag. You can use this accent fabric in small or equally distributed doses for various effects.

Color Recipe Three: Multicolored

If you are going all-out on color, this is easily achieved through purchasing one multicolored fabric that you love. Maybe you'll choose to accent it with a solid-colored fabric or a different print that is more singular in tone to pick up on those same tones in the large multi-print. When mixing two prints together, it's usually nice to make the scale different. For instance, if you were making a skirt out of a large-scale print that had flowers at least 6 or 7 inches in diameter, maybe you would trim it with a band of material that had a small-scale print that isn't floral, like a tiny dot. When creating a quilt or any patchwork item, play with the color in obvious or random ways. You can disperse your colors methodically for the pattern to play out uniformly, or you can do it haphazardly for an unexpected result (perhaps even unexpected by you).

For me, the process of combining color and print has become very much like sitting at an easel and choosing which paint to use next. Sometimes I plan very carefully what I will paint in which color, and other times I'll go at it more like the college painting student in me—fearlessly. Find your style and embrace it. Walking into a fabric store will become like strolling through a box of paints and finding which ones to bring home to your palette. Don't be afraid to make up your own color rules as you go. You may find your own formula for composing colors that will eventually become your trademark. It can happen.

Wash and Wear: Care Considerations

When you embark on your sewing projects, you'll be adding items to your laundry list. There are a few projects in this book, like "Vintage Button Frames" and "Fabric Is Fine Art" in Chapter 8, which you will likely never wash. Therefore, you have the luxury of choosing a fabric only for the appropriate look and weight.

For the other items that you will be washing or dry cleaning, however, you need to consider how the item will be used and see if the care needed suits that use. While the content will give you some clues on how to wash the fabric, many fabrics will have the washing information listed on the bolt. If there is no information on the fabric bolt, always ask and jot down the care instructions if you have to. Some stores will even give you a free care label you could then sew into the item that you've made.

As a rule, you should always wash your fabric before you begin your project. Washing is the first step in sewing before you cut, especially when using fabrics that are mostly made of natural fibers that may shrink. Fabrics that shrink almost always shrink more in length than in width (see the length/width information in the next section). Whether or not you put your new cotton in the dryer will affect how much more it may shrink up. But if you are going to be making a garment from the fabric and will want to both wash and dry it later, you should go ahead and dry it before you sew it up. Some people choose not to put their cottons in the dryer, just like some choose to drip-dry their cotton laundry instead of throwing it in the dryer. An occasional dry cleaning of cotton items that you won't wear often is fine, but too many harsh chemical treatments by a dry cleaner can prove damaging to natural fibers. If you're making a patchwork item, all those fabrics should have already been through the wash individually before you cut and sewed them, and so ideally they will keep their shape just fine. A good pressing will correct your fibers after they've done the tango.

There are several detergents to choose from, and while you may not want to spring any extra cash for something fancy, don't forget the time you've spent creating your amazing project. It may prove well worth it to gently hand-wash that stunning pieced quilt and to do it with a specialty laundry soap intended for fine washables. What you'll need to look for in a hand-wash detergent is how well it will dissolve in cold water and whether it rinses easily. Often, the more upscale fabric stores will offer special detergents for sale, and they'll be all too happy to add them to your stack of fabrics.

Tedious Terms

If you have heard terms like bolt, selvedge, repeat, and nap, yet cannot get a handle on them, this is the section for you. Understanding these terms will teach you the anatomy of fabric and also prove to be a great help when purchasing your fabric and cutting out your patterns.

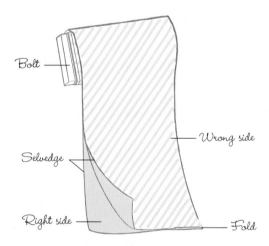

Bolt

Selvedge

Right side

Wrong side

Fold

Bolts of Enlightening

The illustration above shows a bolt of printed fabric that is unrolled a bit. The word *bolt* refers to the flat cardboard form that fabric is wrapped around. Typically the fabric is folded in half, with the right sides facing each other so that the wrong side of the fabric is facing out. This is done to protect the right side. When you are looking through fabric at the store, the bolts are typically standing up on their ends, with a yard or two

of the fabric flipped and turned out so that you can see the right side. When people say a *bolt of fabric,* what they usually are referring to is the standard amount of fabric that is typically on a bolt. This amount varies between 12 and 20 yards, depending on how the store ordered it from the fabric manufacturer. Many home-decorator fabrics (which are typically heavier than the average cotton) and specialty fabrics are not folded and wrapped onto a bolt, but are stored unfolded on longer cylindrical rolls. If you ever special-order fabric in a large quantity, it's nice to get the fabric on a roll so that it's not creased from the folding.

Width Wisdom

Fabric is manufactured in various *widths*. The most common fabric widths are 44/45 inches, 54 inches, and 60 inches. There are a lot of variations on this, such as a specialty embroidered silk that is only 24 inches wide, or cotton broadcloth that is 108 inches wide, suitable for lining a bedspread. The *selvedge* of the fabric refers to the side edges of the fabric, which are the finished, uncut edges. The width of the fabric is determined by measuring the inches from one selvedge across to the other selvedge. You'll notice that the printed varieties will have a narrow, white strip along at least one side, running the entire length of the fabric. This is where the manufacturer's name, and often the fabric designer's name or logo, will appear. It will also have a cute little rainbow of printed circles or squares that will refer to the number of colors used in the printing process. You'll also notice on both selvedges that there are tiny pricked holes that run the entire length of the fabric. These holes are the result of the pins that keep the fabric in place at the factory as it's rolled through several processes. So when you are determining the true width of useable fabric, it should not include the selvedge area that is either unprinted or covered in these tiny holes. The total usable width is usually about 2 inches less than the overall fabric width from edge to edge.

A Lengthy Story

The *length* of the fabric is the measured distance and the direction that runs perpendicular to the width, and parallel to the selvedge of the fabric. The length is the measurement that you will be cutting when you purchase a specific amount. So if you buy 1 yard of 44/45-inch fabric, you will get a cut of fabric that measures 1 yard (36 inches) in length by 44/45 inches in width. Get it? The lengthwise direction of the fabric is also known as the *grain* of the fabric. So the width of the fabric would also be known as the *crossgrain* of the fabric. Think how the lines in wood grain run lengthwise with a plank of hardwood flooring. It's the same for fabric. This is very important when you are cutting out a pattern because the fabric will perform best when it's cut in the correct direction as related to the grain.

Slightly Slanted

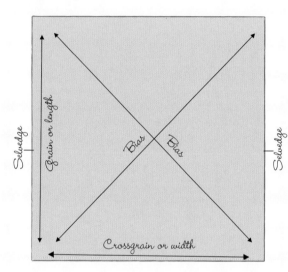

The bias direction of the fabric is at a 45-degree angle to either the grain or the crossgrain of the fabric. As shown in the figure above, it is the diagonal direction of the fabric. The beauty of the bias in a woven material is that there are no threads that are being woven in the bias direction to prevent stretching. So if you take a square of fabric that has been cut squarely on the grain, you can see for yourself, by pulling at opposite diagonal corners, what kind of stretch the bias provides. You'll feel a stretch similar to what a knit can do. The slight difference is that this stretching is also drawing in the other corners as the threads of the material are being pulled in a different direction. So if a bias-cut skirt is too tight, it will pull up the bottom, sometimes unevenly, making it shorter. Therefore, you should pay extra-close attention to leaving enough room in a bias-cut

garment so that it flows freely. When garments are cut on the bias, it is for the advantage of this stretching, but also for the interest that can be created with regard to the print of the fabric. A plaid turned diagonally can sometimes be more flattering than when it is left blocky. Also, a regular stripe takes on a fun diagonal if cut on the bias.

You Should Nap Repeatedly

Prints are often designed so that they can be turned right side up, upside down, or diagonally without making a difference in the look. But some have an up or down to them, for instance, where all the flowers are standing up in one direction. So it'll look upside down if you sew a curtain in the wrong direction. You also wouldn't want the front of a dress to be one way and the back to be the other. The direction of a fabric can also be called the *nap*. The plush fibers in something like a velvet or corduroy will run in one direction or another. The direction of these fibers affects how the fabric feels when you run your hands across it, just like petting an animal the wrong or right way. The direction of the nap also affects how the light hits a fabric—especially something like velvet—which affects the look of the color. Velvet will look like two different fabrics when you take two pieces of the same velvet, turn one upside down, and compare them side by side. So it's important to keep the nap of your fabric consistent when cutting and sewing anything.

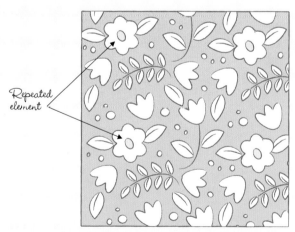

Be aware of *repeats* in your printed fabric (see above) and how to find them both down the length of the fabric and across the width of the fabric; this becomes important if you are seaming together large areas and you want to match up the design so that you don't interrupt it. It's similar to matching up the design in the process of wallpapering. Often a sewing pattern will tell you to buy extra fabric if you are trying to match up a repeat. If you were making a blouse with a horizontal stripe, you would want the stripes to line up together at the side seams.

Yards, Inches, and Quarters

Patterns will typically tell you how much fabric to buy in yards. Whole yards are easy to buy. Often, though, they will read as 1¾ yards or 4⅞ yards or some other fussy fraction. If you're at the counter asking for 8 inches of fabric, they will likely ask you if you want a full ¼ yard, which would be 9 inches. Typically, fabric cutters speak in fractions of a yard, so don't be surprised if they look at you funny when you ask for it in inches or feet. While they should give you the amount you ask for, below is a helpful conversion of yard fractions to inches.

⅛ yard = 4½ inches	⅝ yard = 22½ inches
¼ yard = 9 inches	⅔ yard = 24 inches
⅓ yard = 12 inches	¾ yard = 27 inches
⅜ yard = 13½ inches	⅞ yard = 31½ inches
½ yard = 18 inches	1 yard = 36 inches

Additional considerations when figuring out your yardage will have to do with the width of the particular fabric you've chosen. A yard of a 44-inch-wide fabric will offer you less fabric than 1 yard of a 60-inch-wide fabric. Obvious? Yes, and important to remember. That's why sometimes patterns will have a fabric conversion chart on the back to show you how different your yardage requirements will be, based on the width of your fabric.

The quilting world has inspired an entire industry and language of its own, and so knowing at least a few quilting terms will help you buy fabric. A favorite term to describe a uniquely cut ¼ yard of fabric is a *fat quarter*. It's cut in a way to get the most possible

quilt-shape cuts out of it. Refer to the figures below to see the difference between a regular ¼-yard cut and ¼-yard cut the *fat* way.

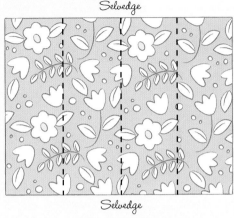

Regular ¼ yard cuts

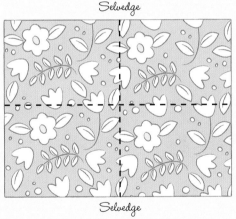

Fat ¼ yard cuts

Notice how 1 yard that is cut on the length in ¼-yard sections produces long, skinny lengths of fabric that are not suitable for anything other than long and skinny things. However, if that yard is cut into fat quarters by making quadrants with the yard, the pieces you are left with are suitable for a pillow, a handbag, a baby dress panel, and tons of other quilting shape options. Quilting stores will offer precut fat quarters for sale. If you want a fat quarter cut from a bolt that you've picked out, you'll actually be buying ½ yard because that's the length that a fat quarter takes up off the bolt. Don't question it, just know it.

Drape

The term *drape* is very often used to describe fabric. What it refers to is the ease with which the fabric *drops* off the body if in the form of clothing, or how it hangs from the table if it's a table linen. Overall, it has to do with the weight and flow of a fabric. Drape describes how the fabric behaves as it covers a person or object and how it takes shape in responding to gravity. If a fabric is stiff, it won't likely have a good drape. If a fabric is weighty and fluid, it will have a very good drape. Sometimes a fabric is just too lightweight to have a good drape because it's not heavy enough to drop well. This matters most when you are making clothing, curtains, bedding, and other less-structured items where there would be a volume of fabric hanging down. A good test of drape at the fabric store is to unroll a few yards, scrunch up a bit of it in your hand, and let a yard or so *waterfall* from your hand. Analyze how the fabric looks hanging down. Are the lines and folds in the fabric long and fluid, or are they more short and stiff looking?

Stash Savvy

Storing your fabric may begin to be a challenge all its own. Depending on the amount you're dealing with and whether or not you want it on display, there are all sorts of storage options.

Just like the ideas I covered in Chapter 1 regarding your sewing room setup, rely on your creative savvy to find cleverness in the chaos of fabric. Use random bookshelves or hutches acquired in flea marketing excursions to stack up your fabrics in the open if you have the space. If you've bought your fabric in a large quantity, like 4 yards or more, it would be perfectly acceptable to ask the store if they have any empty bolts to offer you. Leaving your fabric on the bolt is a good enough way to store it. If you've bought a whole lot of fabric and you're leaving it on long rolls, you can store those standing up in a large metal trashcan, which can be found at a home improvement store. Spray-paint it a fun color and you'll be all design studio-like. Arrange by color, size of print, or type of fabric. Hang several curtain rods, one above the other, on a wall, and let the fabrics fold over the rods, overlapping each other in a beautiful waterfall of color. If you'd rather have them tucked away, then store the smaller cuts in bins and the larger cuts over hangers in a spare closet. Just be sure you are always storing it in a clean, dry, mildew-free area of your home.

Maintain your stash and perhaps *destash* every now and then by sorting through and clipping off oddly shaped, dangling things so that you can fold your fabrics more neatly. Make yourself take on a mini-project every few months by using up some of these small pieces in a craft project, or let the kids have their fun with them. Schedule a swap with your sewing friends where you all bring your unused fabric or the leftovers you've yet to find a project for. You can do this online or on the floor of your best friend's living room with a bottle of wine. At home, make a separate stack of fabrics that are big enough for the front of a pillow but not big enough for a sundress. Keep two separate scrap boxes of the smaller cuts, one for cool colors and one for warm colors. You'll reach for the right thing more quickly when starting any project.

Chapter 4
Sewing School

The following techniques and tutorials are shown in very basic sewing situations with your sewing machine, but with practice you'll be on your way to more advanced applications. You also can refer back to these techniques when you start sewing the

projects. This is only one girl's way to sew! Finding your own way will likely end up being a combination of influences. This is where about 30 years of self-guided sewing has brought me—a place where simple and traditional techniques are welcome.

Stitches, Notches, Nips, and Clips

Once you've gotten to know your sewing machine, you'll want to play around with all the different stitch types, stitch lengths, stitch widths, tension settings, and so on. Most likely, the manual that came with your machine will help you through this process. If not, take a sewing class or have a sewing friend or family member spend a day with you and your new machine.

Stitches

Every sewing application has its own ideal stitch setting that includes the stitch type, stitch length, and the tension setting for that particular stitch. The straight stitch is the most basic stitch style to create seams, hems, and topstitching, among other tasks. The longer (higher number) you have your stitch length set to, the longer each individual stitch will be. A machine-basting stitch is essentially a straight stitch set at its longest stitch length. Because basting stitches are not small and tight, they are easy to remove later and are thought of

as temporary stitches, or foundation stitches, before moving onto final stitches.

A shorter stitch length (lower number) creates a more durable seam, simply due to the increased quantity of stitches. Shorter stitches are a good choice when sewing on curves. Somewhere in the middle of long and short is a good choice for seams, hemstitching, and topstitching.

In the ideal stitch, both the top thread and the bobbin thread are being pulled into the fabric equally and are linking within the fibers of the fabric. If the bobbin loops are visible from the topside, or the top thread loops are visible on the underside, chances are your tension is not set right.

Tension is an important factor in achieving good stitch quality. The tension controls how tightly the thread is drawn into the fabric as it feeds through the machine and creates interlinking stitches. A tension set too tightly (high) will pucker your fabric or cause the thread to break in the machine. If the tension is set too loosely (low), then the stitches won't be secure. Getting the tension just right ensures that you will have smooth and secure seams with no puckers. After you've checked to ensure that your machine is threaded properly, both the tension and the stitch-length settings are the main variables to play with when troubleshooting your stitch quality. You also need to take the fabric type into consideration when choosing your tension settings. Every now and then, a different type of thread may also have you making some minor adjustments to your settings.

Backstitching is essentially just stitching in reverse, and it's good to do ½ inch or so right over your straight stitches at the beginning and end of every seam, unless otherwise noted in the pattern you are following. It basically knots the thread for you. You can also create a lockstitch without backstitching by setting your stitch length to zero and letting it stitch in place for a few stitches.

The zigzag stitch is likely the next most important basic stitch on your machine. It's ideal for finishing the raw edges of fabric if you don't have a serger. Zigzag stitches are also a great stitch to use when easing on elastic, and hemming knit fabrics. When using a zigzag stitch, you'll not only be able to set the stitch length and tension, but you will also need to set the stitch width. The width will determine how wide the z's are in your zigzag.

Notches and Nips

If you're familiar with sewing from patterns, then you are familiar with the *notch* symbol, which often appears on the edges of patterns like little triangles either in single or double width. These notches are visual clues to help illustrate where pattern pieces will come together, to point out the center of a garment piece, or to assure you as you sew that you have the pieces lined up correctly.

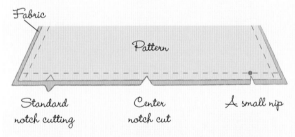

Fabric

Pattern

Standard notch cutting   Center notch cut   A small nip

There are a few methods to mark these notches on your pattern, which can include cutting the notch shape out, nipping with your scissors, or simply marking with chalk on the outer edge. While I admit to sometimes ignoring notches, if a pattern has several pieces that could get confused or if you've never sewn with the pattern before it's a good idea to mark notches. The figure above shows how to cut around a typical pattern notch and also a center notch. With a pattern notch you cut around the triangle on the outward edge of your pattern and with a center notch you should cut into the seam allowance of the piece just a bit. These are cut differently so that they are not confused with one

another. Be careful to only use the tip of your scissors when cutting into the seam allowance to avoid cutting more than you want to cut.

Making short nips on the outside edges of your pattern pieces with just the point of your scissors is a good way to show where a stitch line starts, stops or turns. Nipping is best done when a pattern uses ⅝-inch seam allowances, so that there is room to make your nips without going too close to the stitch line. You also wouldn't want to make the nips deeper than about ¼ inch. Other good places to nip a pattern in the seam allowances are where a zipper should stop, the center point of a sleeve, where darts are placed, where pockets are sewn into a side seam and where hems turn up at the seams.

Clips

Clipping your seam allowance is also very important after sewing curved seams and seams that have corners. In areas like neck lines, armholes, the curve of a hip, or the corners of a pillow, clipping helps the seams to lie smoothly once they are turned right side out. When clipping you would want to stay about ⅛ inch away from the stitching, taking great care not to clip through it. When clipping an outer curved seam, like the bottom curve of a Peter Pan collar, or a circular pillow it's best to not only clip, but also to cut out a wedge shape or *wedge clip*, similar to how you make a center notch cut. When clipping an interior curve, you can just make snips in the seam allowance. When clipping corners, you would just snip off the exterior corner of the seam allowance at a 45-degree angle. All three of these clip examples are shown in the figure below.

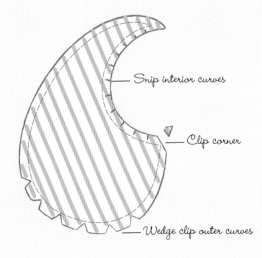

Snip interior curves

Clip corner

Wedge clip outer curves

Seams to You

There is more than one way to join two pieces of fabric together—many different seam styles are appropriate for different situations. You do not have to own a serger to get a nice, finished seam allowance. In many of the projects in this book, the seams will not be exposed at all, and so not all of the instructions include finishing the seams. In sewing garments that get a frequent washing, it's good to finish off the seams to keep them durable and fray-free. The following are simple explanations of various seam types and seam finishes.

Encased Seams
Bound Seam

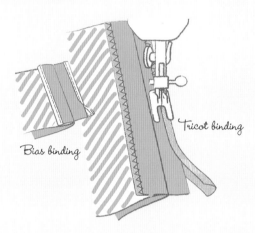

Tricot binding

Bias binding

In order to totally encase the edges of your seam allowances, you can wrap bias strips or *tricot strips* around the edges and sew a single line of stitching that catches both the top and the bottom of the strip with the seam allowance sandwiched in between. Pre-folded bias in a package is only recommended for heavier-weight materials, such as for coats. Lightweight and sheet tricot strips, folded lengthwise, are recommended for lighter-weight fabrics. When sewing on tricot strips, you can use an unfinished tricot edge, and cut on the grain, stretching it slightly as you sew with it and using a zigzag stitch.

Self-Bound Seam

This seam finishing is a good one to do on the garments where you forgot to come up with a finishing option until after you started sewing. Not that I've ever done that. Ahem.

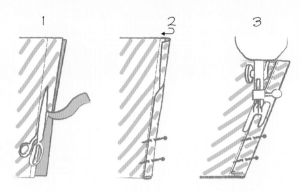

1 Begin with a ⅝-inch seam allowance, and do not press open. Trim one side of the seam allowance to ⅛ inch from the stitch line.

2 Fold the remaining seam allowance over twice toward the trimmed seam allowance so that the finished fold edge covers the trimmed edge of the first seam allowance and is snug up against the stitch line.

3 Stitch down the folded edge as close as possible to the first line of stitching, only going through the seam allowances. Press to one side.

French Seam

Parlez-vous perfect seams? This is a great seam option with very professional results, but it is best used on generally straight seams. You may have to re-train your brain to begin by sewing *wrong sides* of the fabric together first.

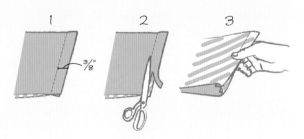

1 Start by sewing the *wrong* sides using a ⅜-inch seam allowance.

2 Trim the seam allowance down to ⅛ inch, and fold back to the *right* sides with the stitch line exactly in the fold. Press flat, keeping the stitch line in the fold.

3 Now sew again, keeping the *right* sides together at a ¼-inch seam allowance, thereby encasing the first seam allowance and its edges within the second seam.

Other Seam Finishes

The following is list of additional ways to finish seams:

- A **stitched and pinked** finish can be done after you've made the seam. Simply sew a straight stitch along the outer edge of each side of the seam allowance, ¼ inch away from the unfinished edge. Then trim with pinking shears as close to the edge stitching as you can, taking care to not snip through it.

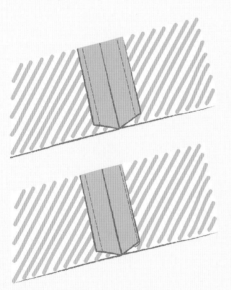

- To make a **turned and stitched** finish, sew a seam as you normally would and press open. Then sew through each side of the seam allowance only, about ⅛ inch away from the unfinished edge. Then fold the seam allowances back with the stitch lines in the fold, and stitch again, only through the seam allowance, one side at a time. Press again.

- To make a **zigzag** finish, set your zigzag stitch width to the widest setting and at a pretty short stitch length. Before sewing your pattern pieces together, finish the edges of them with a zigzag stitch made very close to the edge without going over the edge. Sew your seams and press open. You can then go back and trim the excess seam

allowance from the outside of the zigzag stitch, being careful not to clip through it. This finishing technique will be used for some of the garment projects in Part II.

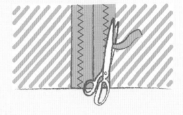

You can also finish the edges with a zigzag stitch that intentionally goes right over the edge, thereby binding the edge of the seam allowance. Align your fabric's edge under the sewing foot so that it passes just to the left of the needle as it comes down on the *right* side of the zigzag stitch so that the needle misses the edge. You may need to loosen the tension on your dial to prevent the fabric from puckering when making this type of finish.

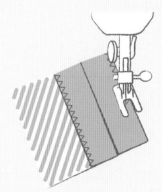

Zippity Hoorah: The Centered Zipper

There are sewers who have been sewing for years but avoid garments with zippers in them out of fear. Fear not! There are many methods to sewing in a zipper, each suited for different purposes. The three main methods are the centered zipper, the lapped zipper, and the invisible zipper. Since I'll use the centered zipper method to install a zipper in the "Doggie Dreams Bed" project in Chapter 9, that's the method I'll cover here. This is probably the easiest and most straightforward method, and is perfect for adding zippers to cushion covers or pillow covers for easy removal for washing. This particular centered zipper method employs a few extra techniques to ensure that the zipper is secure and won't buckle the fabric. If you already know how to do this—zip it and move on.

1   Pre-wash your fabrics, and also soak the zipper in hot water for a few minutes and allow it to dry.

2   Stitch the seam that your zipper will go on at ⅝ inch from the edge, but only machine-baste (long stitches) in the length of the seam that will have the zipper on it. (It's a good idea to have first cut the fabric edges with pinking shears, or have them finished with a zigzag stitch or serging to prevent fraying.)

3   Cut two strips of lightweight fusible interfacing about an inch wide and as long as the zipper. Press the seam allowances to the left, place one of the strips centered lengthwise over the basting stitches, and press into place following the interfacing's directions. Switch sides by pressing both seam allowances to the right, and repeat.

4   Now press the seam open well and pin the *right* side of the zipper against the seam allowances only, with the head of the zipper extended beyond the top edge of the fabric. This is why you should purchase zippers that are a few inches longer than you need. Check as you pin to be sure you are lining the center combs of the zipper along the seam line.

5   Attach the zipper foot to your machine as directed by your machine's manual. Machine-baste from top to bottom, just through the zipper tape and the seam allowance. Repeat on the other side from top to bottom.

6   Turn the fabric to the *right* side and topstitch through all layers ⅜ inch away from the center seam from the bottom up on each side. You may also want to run a horizontal stitch line across the bottom end of the zipper. (It may be helpful to mark your stitch lines ahead of time with chalk.)

7   Now use a seam ripper to carefully cut the basting stitches from Step 2, and remove them to expose the zipper teeth. Remove the loose threads.

8   Slide the zipper head down within the fabric area, clip the extra tape off, and hem the top, as directed by your particular pattern.

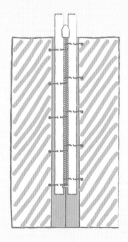

Step 4

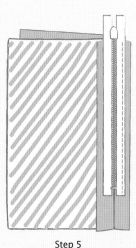

Step 5

Pipe Dream

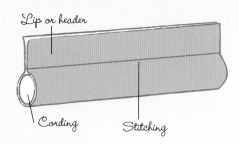

Lip or header

Cording   Stitching

As shown in the figure above, piping consists of a band of fabric (usually bias-cut), wrapped around a soft, rope-like length, called *cording*, and stitched together. The header would be carefully sewn into a seam so that the piping stitching doesn't show. Hefty piping is a wonderful accent around pillows and cushions, while tiny piping is sweet on the edges of children's clothing or edging the pockets of a vintage-style apron.

When you are sandwiching piping between two layers of fabric you need to be careful because you have to stitch close enough to the piping to make sure that its stitch line isn't visible once it's turned out. Therefore, when using piping or cording around a pillow, you should baste the piping to one fabric layer first, and then stitch all layers together afterward.

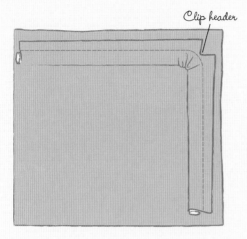

Clip header

When sewing the piping around the corners, you should clip the header of the piping to help it make a smooth turn around the corners (see figure above). If you are using piping to go around corners and around curves, you should always use piping that is made with bias-cut material. This will ensure smooth turns and keep the piping from wrinkling or bunching up. While there are methods to make continuous piping that joins seamlessly where the end meets the beginning on something like a pillow, I've always found that overlapping the two ends, each at a gradual angle toward the seam allowance, is just as good.

Here's how you can make your own piping:

1   To determine the width your fabric strips need to be, wrap a tape measure around the cording, letting the end of the tape measure extend out well past the cording by about ½ inch or so. Where the tape end hits will be the measurement

reading for the width of the fabric. If you have an especially fat cording, you should allow a little extra width.

2   The best way to cut fabric strips for piping is on the bias. Skip ahead to the "Maybe I'm Bias" tutorial on the next page to learn how to cut and join bias strips correctly.

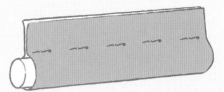

Step 3

3   Once you've joined enough lengths of bias strips together for the desired length of your piping, wrap them around the cord snugly and pin them in place. (Skip the pinning if it makes your sewing more comfortable.)

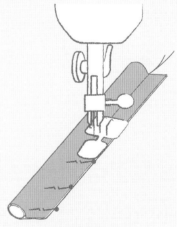

Step 4

4   Stitch the seam allowances together to encase the cording using a zipper foot. Let the cording push up against the side of the zipper foot snugly.

Note: One trick I like to use, especially when the piping will go on garments, is to use yarn in place of cording when making the piping. I find it much more supple and easy to sew with than cording, which can be a little stiff for garment sewing.

A Small Gathering

It's likely that your sewing machine either came with, or has the option to add, a gathering foot or ruffler foot that will help you make all the ruffles you could ever want. I've included my little gathering technique here for the rest of you. It's a technique that I continue to use because I think I secretly like laborious details. I also find that even though you can set the gathering ratios for your machine ruffler, it isn't always accurate. So I feel that I can control the fullness of my gathers better by hand. This lesson will help you gather ruffles for the "Bo Peep Skirt" project in Chapter 7 and countless other fancies.

1   On the *right* side of the fabric and leaving a thread tail of about 6 inches, begin machine-basting (long stitches) about ½ inch away from the side edge of your fabric and about ¼ inch away from the top edge. Continue stitching, keeping at ¼ inch from the edge and ending about ½ inch away from the other side edge. Do not backstitch or knot your fabric at the beginning or the end of this stitching. Leave a thread tail of about 6 inches.

2   Repeat Step 1, at about ⅛ inch lower than the first stitch line, to form two even rows of basting.

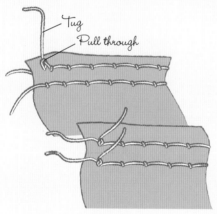

Step 3

3   On one side of the fabric, tug on the top thread tail of the top row, enough to draw up the bobbin thread, and pull through. Knot the top and bobbin threads together. Repeat on the basting row below.

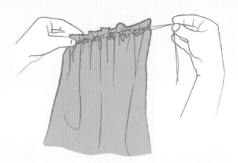

Step 4

4   On the opposite end, pick up the top threads only of both of the basting rows, and begin to tug on them gently away from the fabric with one hand, while you're drawing the fabric into a gather with the other hand. This motion is somewhat similar to treating the top threads like a drawstring.

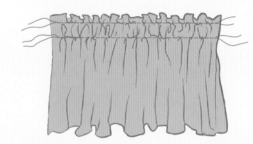

Step 5

5   Gently continue in this fashion until you have decreased the width of the fabric and created the desired fullness of gathers. Trim your drawstrings back to about 6 inches or so, and knot them together with the bobbin threads.

6   Gently smooth out the gathers until they are even, and move on to your next sewing step.

Note: You don't have to use two rows of basting stitches to do this, but it comes greatly recommended. It's insurance if one of your threads should break, and it's easier to get the gathers to lie flat along the edge for the rest of the sewing steps when there are two rows. This is especially true if you are gathering a long pass of fabric.

Maybe I'm Bias

As explained in Chapter 3, there are many advantages, both in the design and fit, to making garments that are cut on the bias. Bias strips are also the number-one choice when binding the edges of a quilt. I'll also use bias strips for the details of the "Prairie Blouse" project in Chapter 7. The first thing to learn about bias strips is how to cut them correctly. If they are mistakenly cut at any angle other than a perfect 45 degrees, their ability to curve will be inconsistent and will cause rippling. The steps are simple, and once you've tried it, it'll be easy to do it again.

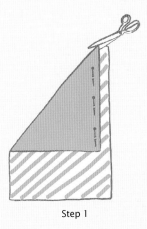

Step 1

1   Fold your fabric so that the straight cut along the crossgrain of the fabric is parallel to the selvedge of the fabric. This will form a right triangle, as shown above. You may want to pin the cut edge next to the selvedge to keep the angle in place.

2   Cut the fabric along the fold-line to establish your true bias line. You could press a crease in this line first if it helps, but take care not to stretch the fold out of its 45-degree angle with the iron.

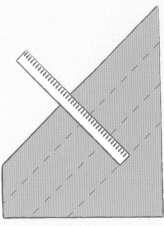

Step 3

3   Using the first cut line as your guide to measure from, you can continue to mark with chalk and cut successive bias lines. Just make sure that all your strips are consistently equal in width.

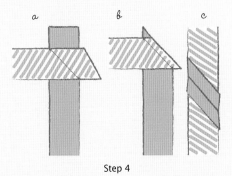

Step 4

4   When you need to make a long bias strip, you can join several together. Do this by laying two strips *right* sides together at a right angle. Sew them together between their overlapping intersections at an angle (a). Trim the allowance to ¼ inch (b). Press open, and trim the tips even with the bias edges (c).

Be Edge-y

Now what do you do with all those bias strips? Oh, so many things! Here are the instructions for binding a quilt with them and for edging a garment.

Quilt Binding

You would perform the following binding steps after the quilt has been backed and quilted either by machine or by hand. In other words, this is the very last process in finishing a quilt.

1   For a finished binding that is ⅞-inch wide, you'll need to cut the bias strips 4¼-inches wide. Measure the perimeter of your quilt. Using the instructions from the tutorial, "Maybe I'm Bias," cut and join as many bias strips as necessary to go around the entire perimeter of your quilt, plus about 18 inches.

2 At one end of the bias that is cut at a 45-degree angle, fold back about ½ inch toward the *wrong* side and press a crease.

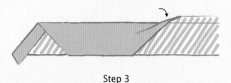

Step 3

3 Now fold and press the bias strip in half lengthwise throughout the entire length to form a nice crease.

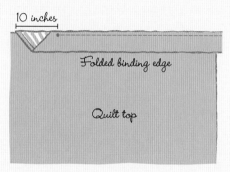

10 inches

Folded binding edge

Quilt top

Step 4

4 On the *right* side of the quilt, and starting in the middle of any side of the quilt, lay the pressed end of the binding down first, and line up the raw edges of the binding with the raw edges of your quilt. Begin sewing through all layers, about 10 or 11 inches from the end of the binding at a ¼-inch seam allowance.

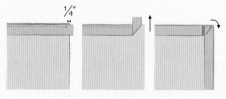

¼"

Step 5

5 Continue sewing and stop ¼ inch away from the corner edge. Backstitch and clip the threads. Fold the binding at a right angle away from the quilt,

forming an angled fold. Then fold it back down again in the opposite way, forming a straight fold that is in line with the sewn edge of the quilt. Pin or hold in place.

6 Begin sewing again down the next edge, starting ¼ inch away from the fold of the binding and the edge of the quilt.

7 Repeat Steps 4 and 5 on the other three corners of the quilt.

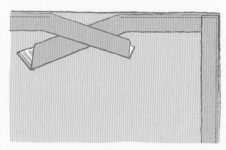

Step 8

8 Stop sewing when you are about 12 inches away from where you began sewing the binding to the quilt.

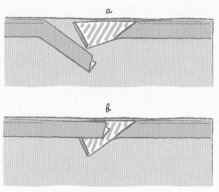

a

b

Step 9

9 Now open the fold of the pressed end of the binding that you began with (a). Lay the other end of the binding inside the fold of the first (b).

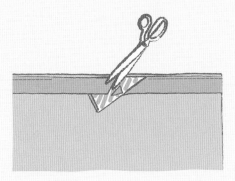

Step 10

10 Cut the end of the binding that is lying inside the other at a 45-degree angle that is opposite from the pressed binding's angle, an inch or two away from the pressed binding's edge.

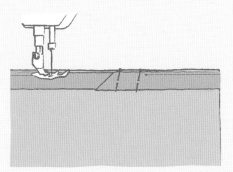

Step 11

11 Now fold the pressed binding back up to smoothly encase the cut one, and pin all layers in place. Finish sewing through all layers at a ¼-inch seam allowance to join the stopping and starting points of your sewing. (You can go back and blind-sew this overlapping joint together when you do the finishing stitching. Refer to the "Sewing Blind" tutorial in Chapter 5.)

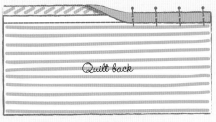

Step 12

12 Turn the binding up to the edge of the quilt and then fold down onto the other side, just enough to cover your stitching line, and so that the width of the binding on each side is equal. Pin in place.

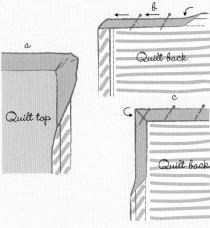

Step 13

13 At the corners of the *right* side, you'll notice when you turn your binding up toward the edge that a nice, mitered corner has been formed (a). You can also create this same mitered corner on the back side. With the back of the quilt facing you, fold down the binding to cover the stitch line and smooth this fold all the way beyond the edge of the quilt (b). This will make the binding form an angled fold at the corner. Simply turn this angle back in toward the quilt to cover the next side's stitching, and you will have formed the mitered corner. Pin in place (c).

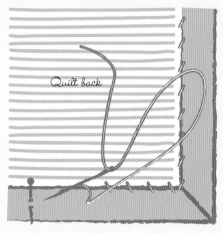

Step 14

14 Now begins the relaxing task of blind-sewing the binding down to the backing by hand. While you could use the machine to perform topstitching instead, it's not recommended. It is difficult to manage the bulk of a quilt, to keep your sewing line straight, and to make sure you are catching the binding on both the top and bottom all at once. Not to mention that a hand-sewn edge looks much nicer. At least I think so.

Decorative Binding on Garment Edges

Sewing bias edges onto garments, tote bags, dog leashes, aprons, blankets, and more is so absolutely charming that it's easy to get carried away. It's also a fantastic way to jazz up a plain purchased item with a pretty printed edge. It's very, very adorable on hand towels and table linens. Just be sure to wash and press both the item and the fabric you'll be cutting the bias strips from before you begin.

You can use the following instructions when sewing a bias binding to a sleeve cuff, the hem of pants, skirt, blouse, the neckline, etc. These instructions take the place of edge finishing or hemming instructions. However, unlike turning an edge up and hemming, it will not decrease the length of the item, but will keep it the same. So keep this in mind when figuring your finished lengths. In the method described here, the finished binding width will be one-quarter of the cut binding width. So if you

want the finished binding width to be ½ inch, then you'll need to cut the binding 2 inches wide.

1 Once your item has all the seams sewn together and pressed, you can finish the edge with a bias binding. Measure the circumference of the edge you'd like to bind. Using the "Maybe I'm Bias" tutorial, cut bias strips and join them if necessary to form a strip that is at your desired width and just a few inches longer than your circumference. Cut the ends bluntly.

2 Fold the strip in half lengthwise, *wrong* sides together, and press. Then fold each of the edges in once more to meet the center crease, and press again on each side. Your bias strip should now be folded equally into four lengthwise sections divided by the three creases.

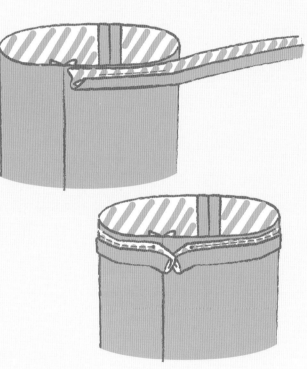

Step 3

3 Start about 2 inches from the strip's end and near a seam of the garment. Open up the folds of the strip. With *right* sides together and unfinished edges aligned, sew the bias strip to the garment edge in the top crease all the way around, and stop about 2 inches from where you started.

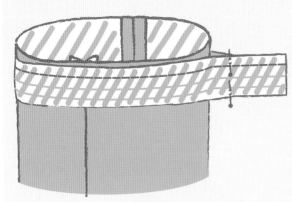

Step 4

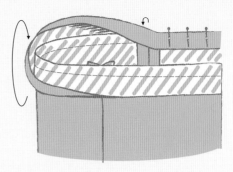

Step 7

4 Lay the item out in front of you so that the remaining binding edges are lying on top of each other, extending out past the edge of the garment. With your hands, press the garment down into a folded edge in the space where the strips are not sewn on. Now pin the loose bias strips together, right where they first meet beyond the garment, without going through it.

5 Join the strips together with a straight stitch on your pin line, being careful not to sew through the garment during this step. Trim the seam allowance of the binding to ½ inch or so.

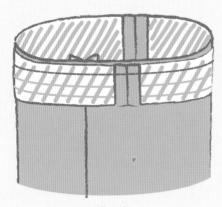

Step 6

6 Open up the binding seam allowance and continue sewing in the top fold of the bias to join the rest of it to the garment's edge, joining the starting and stopping points from Step 3.

7 Now fold the *wrong* side of the binding up toward the garment's edge, and then fold again back down toward the inside of the garment. The center fold of the binding should be right on the top edge of the seam allowance. The third fold in the binding should lie right on, or right next to, the binding stitch line, concealing the binding's edges and all the seam allowances. Pin in place (or not).

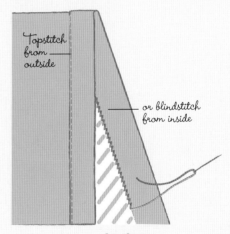

Topstitch from outside

or blindstitch from inside

Step 8

8 Now you can hand-sew a blind stitch or topstitch on the machine to finish the binding. If you topstitch on the machine, do so from the *right* side of the binding just inside the binding's sewn-on edge, and be sure you are catching the inner edge as well. Topstitching from the outside will allow you to keep your stitches even on the visible side of the garment.

Chapter 5

By Hand

This chapter offers some simple and simply ingenious little hand-sewing techniques that I find myself using again and again. You may already have some of your own versions of the techniques, but I, for one, always appreciate seeing how other people

do the same thing. I wanted to nest several of these goodies all in one spot for easy reference later on in the book, and for later on in your life. Good techniques inspire greatly; pass them on.

Hole-y Buttons

Have you every heard someone say they can't even sew on a button? This is for them, so buy them a copy of this book or share when you're done. As basic as it may sound, there is a right and not-so-right way to sew on a button.

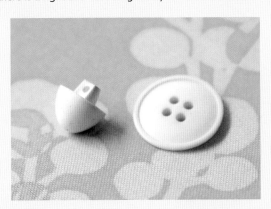

You can see the two types of buttons above—the *shank* button (left) and the *sew-through* button. The shank button is designed to leave room between the underside of the button and the fabric it's sewn onto to accommodate the second layer of fabric that will be there

once it's buttoned. When sewing with a sew-through button, you need to create the shank with thread to leave room for that extra layer of fabric underneath.

Sewing on a Sew-Through Button

If you sew a sew-through button too tightly against the cloth, it may be hard to use. You do not need to sew a shank, if you are sewing buttons on for completely decorative purposes.

1   Thread the needle with a double layer of thread, and knot.

2   Mark the center location of your button placement with a washable fabric marker dot.

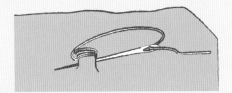

Step 3

3   Come up through the fabric from the wrong side, and make a few backstitches to anchor the thread in place.

4   Center your button over the anchoring stitches, and come up with the needle through one of the holes.

Step 5

5   Now place a toothpick on top of the button between the buttonholes, and make your stitches up and down through the holes and over the toothpick several times, alternating sides. It doesn't make a difference whether you do this with a four-hole or two-hole button, nor does it matter whether or not you cross your threads. The technique will be the same.

Step 6

6   Slide the toothpick out. Pull up on the button a bit, and stitch once more down through the button, but not through the fabric. Now wind the thread around the vertical threads several times tightly, and stitch back down through the fabric next to the shank that you've created.

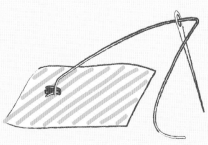

Step 7

7   On the underside, instead of making a fat knot, make a tunnel of stitches. Make several backstitches next to each other, and then put your needle underneath them and pull through on the thread. Clip the thread close to the tunnel. Be sure that these stitches are not sewn from the top, but are hidden under the button.

Sewing on a Shank Button

Shank buttons are a little dressier than sew-through buttons, since you don't see the thread they are sewn on with. They are ideal when you are using thick fabrics like wool or denim. You'll notice how, on a heavy coat, a shank button sort of dangles downward a bit when not buttoned, but stays in place when it is buttoned.

1   Follow Steps 1, 2, and 3 for the sew-through button technique.

2   With your needle and thread on top of the fabric, place the shank of the button right next to where the thread is coming out.

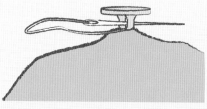

Step 3

3   Put your needle through the shank, and in one stitch motion, stitch underneath the shank and through the fabric to come out on the top side of the fabric again on the other side of the shank.

4   Once you've repeated this stitch several times, follow Step 7 for the sew-through button technique to knot your thread.

Loop-de-Loop

There are several ways to make a buttonhole, both automatically on your machine and by hand. I'll leave the machine buttonholes to you and your sewing machine manual. Making tiny loops with elastic, roll-hemmed fabric, and ribbon are also great alternatives to the standard buttonhole. I want to show you one more of my favorite little button loops, also known as a *thread eye*. This is the recommended button loop for the "Right Off the Cuff" project in Chapter 7. It's so simple and delicate, yet durable, and it is like crocheting with thread. Does that sound hard? It's not. Here we go.

1   Once you've sewn on the button that you'll be using, you can begin to make the button loop on the opposing panel of the garment. Lay out both

sides next to each other in line, to mark where your button loop should stop and start. Pin in those two areas, lining the pins up with the width of your button.

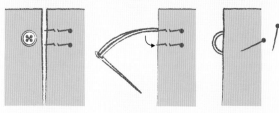

Steps 1 and 2

2 At the edge of the fabric that you want to make the loop, insert a double-threaded needle from underneath, through the edge, and out at one of the pin points. Return the needle back into edge at the point of the other pin. Don't pull your slack all the way through, but leave an open loop there. The length of the loop will be determined by how big your button is. Remove the pins.

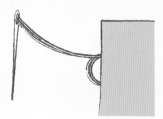

Step 3

3 Repeat Step 2 in the same points at the edge so that there is now a four-strand loop. Send the needle out through the starting point again.

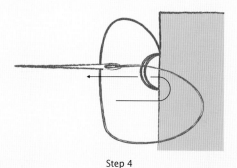

Step 4

4 The loops are now a foundation that you will work blanket stitches around. Begin by sending the needle through the loop from the top down, and passing the needle over the top of the slack before you pull tightly. Continue until you have several blanket stitches snugly against one another covering the foundation of the loop.

Step 5

5 Take a few small, securing stitches underneath, and then knot and trim the threads.

Run Along Now
Running Stitch

We have every kind of machine possible to replicate the simple running stitch for us, but nothing can replace the human touch that is visible in even the most perfect of handmade running stitches. Made with hands, they are easy, yet highly functional, naïve yet refined. Slow? Yes. Sound like a little too much to describe such a tiny thing? No. The running stitch is like sketching in the fine art of sewing. It's an extremely charming addition if stitched decoratively with embroidery floss along the edge of a hem, cuff, collar, or blanket.

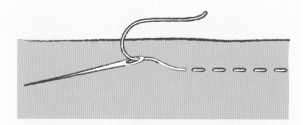

If you were to piece a quilt top by hand, it could be with this stitch. After aligning the edges of your pieces, you'd want to make your stitches very close together, and evenly spaced from each other and from the edge. This would also be the style of stitch that you would most likely use to quilt the layers of a quilt together in either a patterned direction or along some of the pieced edges of your quilt top.

Whip stitch

A *whip stitch* is as quick and strong as it sounds, and is also referred to as an *overcast stitch*. It has a lot of uses, but is mostly used when you want to bind an edge and at the same time sew two pieces of fabric together. This makes it a good option for sewing down any rolled edge against itself. If you are careful, you can make this stitch invisible from the outside, which makes it great for hems. Here are a few tips to whip it good. The following will detail how to whip stitch a rolled hem.

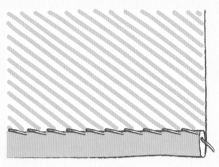

Step 3

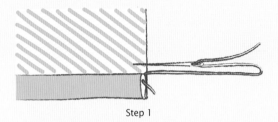

Step 1

1   Bring the needle up from underneath through the rolled edge, letting the knotted tail stay between the rolled top and the bottom layer. In line with the rolled edge but into the bottom layer, catch just a few fibers on the tip of your needle to prevent the stitch from being visible from the other side.

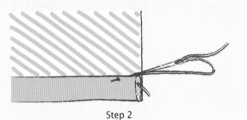

Step 2

2   Now, before pulling the needle out all the way, insert it into the rolled edge and stitch through it about ¼ inch before pulling the thread through.

3   Continue this stitch, catching just a few bottom fabric fibers again before returning into the rolled edge for another ¼-inch stitch. Repeat over and over until you've reached the end. Backstitch and knot into the rolled edge. With a lot of practice, the process of angling over toward the bottom fabric to grab a few fibers invisibly, and back toward the rolled edge for a ¼-inch stitch, can be made in almost a single motion.

Sewing Blind

Whether you call it a *slip stitch*, a *blind stitch*, an *appliqué stitch*, or an *invisible stitch*, the idea is that it's a sneaky little stitch that does not show from the outside. It's perfect for appliquéing fabric shapes to a quilt top or closing the open side of a pillow. A slightly different version of this stitch is also how you'll finish your quilt binding in the "Playing Along Quilt" project in Chapter 8, as well as the "Here's the Dish Towel" project in Chapter 9.

The following instructions detail how you would stitch a pillow closed.

1   Once both sides of the opening have been pressed toward the wrong side, and the pillow form has been inserted, pin the opening closed.

2   Knot your long, single-threaded needle, and insert it, from underneath, inside one of the folds at the end. Now directly across and through the other fold, insert the needle through only a single layer of the fold and in a direction going away from where you started, and come out through the fold, about ¼ inch away.

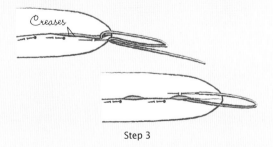

Creases

Step 3

3 Repeat now on the other side, and continue throughout the whole length of the pillow, removing the pins as you go. The stitches will look the smoothest if you are sure to keep entering and exiting the needle through the very crease of the folds.

An Invisible Variation

This version is what I would consider a true appliqué stitch. The only difference is that, instead of joining two folded edges together, you are joining one folded edge down to a flat surface. This method can also be called *needle turn appliqué* because as you sew, you can use the tip of your needle to turn the fabric's edge under just before you sew it down.

Once your appliquéd shape has smooth, folded edges, pin it in place and begin the stitching, just as you did in the previous tutorial, by bringing the needle first through the fold. Just be sure when you take your short stitch into the bottom fabric that you are doing so directly underneath the very outer edge of the piece you are sewing down. Some people prefer to do appliqué with their fabric in an embroidery hoop.

Super Circles

I named this method *Super Circles* because, after my friend Kathy Doughty taught it to me, I was feeling like a sewing superhero. This is a simple technique for getting a smooth fold on a curve, which is very helpful for making fancy shapes for appliqué, like in the "Here's the Dish Towel" in Chapter 9, and everyday items, like a pocket with curved corners. Get your iron and some aluminum foil, and maybe get some popcorn while you're at it.

1 Determine the shape and size of the circle, pocket, or other curved shape that you'd like to get a neat fold on, and draw and cut it from poster board. Take special care to make the cut smooth and neat. Cut the fabric out in the same shape, but with an extra ½ inch or so all around the perimeter.

Step 2

2 Lay down a modest length of foil, then your fabric shape *right* side down, and then your poster-board shape centered in the middle. Fold the foil down toward the center of the shape all the way around, letting the fabric fold in tightly with it. Smooth the edges of the shape with your fingers.

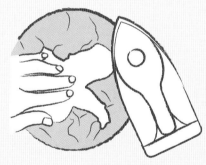

Step 3

3 Now press down the foil all along the outer edges with your iron on a medium-high, non-steam setting. Turn over and repeat. Be careful—it gets quite hot!

4 After letting it cool for just a bit, peel back the foil and remove it. Now carefully remove the poster board from inside the creased edges. Your perfectly folded piece is all ready for sewing onto its final resting spot.

Simply Stitch-y

The following embroidery stitches are those that everyone should know how to do. Just because. Embroidery is a wonderful way to pass the time if you should actually have some time, and even better when you don't. Making your own drawings on fabric with an air- or water-soluble pen is the perfect way to stitch a work of art. Simply hand-sew along your hand-drawn or traced lines in your desired colors with some of the stitches described below. You'll use a few of these to embellish your "Here's the Dish Towel" project in Chapter 9, so get out the hoops and let's practice.

Split Stitch

The split stitch forms a nice, neat, solid line in embroidery that you can compare to drawing with thread. It's great for outlining appliqués, and several concentric rows of split stitches can create good fill-in for embroidery designs. At least four strands of embroidery floss are recommended to perform this stitch. After you've brought the needle up and pulled the slack all the way through, follow these next steps.

1   Following your desired line, and with the needle angled back toward the starting point, insert the needle through about ¼ inch away from the starting point and immediately back out again, just a hair farther, thus taking a tiny backstitch.

2   Before pulling the needle and thread through, aim the needle through the middle of the strands just as they come out of the starting point. Pull the thread and needle through now until it's nice and taught, and so that it creates the beginning of an interlinking stitch line.

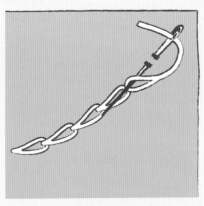

Step 3

3   Now repeat Steps 1 and 2 until you have your desired length. Knot underneath, weave back through some of the underneath stitching, and trim the threads.

Chain Stitch

The chain stitch is somewhat similar to the split stitch but is slightly loopier. Just like the split stitch, the chain stitch can be used to form flowing and curved lines of any kind. There are several versions of the chain stitch, and the following steps create what is considered to be the basic chain stitch. After you've brought the needle up and pulled the slack all the way through, follow these next steps.

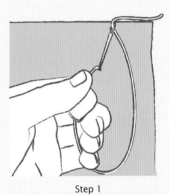

Step 1

1   Hold down the thread a tiny amount where it just came out from the fabric, using the thumb on the opposite hand you sew with. Insert the needle back into the hole it came up through, continuing to hold the thread down as you pull through so that the stitch doesn't slip all the way back through.

Step 2

2   While there is still a loop left on top, poke the needle back up and through the loop to catch it, and pull the thread through.

Step 3

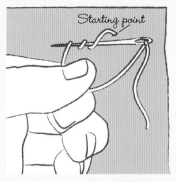

Step 1

3 Now with the needle facing the line you are following, insert the needle right next to where you just came out of and then back through the top a short distance away. Keep the needle above your slack as you pull through to form the next loop. Repeat this step until you're finished.

1 Hold the needle right above where the thread is emerging from the fabric, and use your opposite hand to wrap the base of the thread around the needle tip two or three times, not letting go of the thread after you've wrapped it.

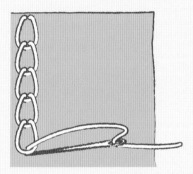

Step 4

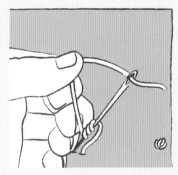

Step 2

4 At the end, insert the needle straight down on the other side of the last loop you've made to anchor it. Knot underneath, weave back through some of the underneath stitching, and trim the threads.

French Knot

Is there a cuter knot? I think knot! I'm not sure what's so French about this, maybe the twist, but I simply adore this tiny and friendly embellishment. After you've brought the needle up exactly where you want the knot to be, and pulled the slack all the way through, follow these next steps.

2 Now, still holding the thread taught, move the tip of the needle point back to the base where you first brought the needle up, and insert it right next to (but not into) the hole you came up from. As you do this, the twist of the thread on the needle should tighten as you continue to hold the thread taught with the other hand.

3 Pull the thread all the way through, only leaving a little knot on the surface. Continue as many times as you wish!

Part
2 Projects

Chapter 6
Organize

Cozy Cubes

These cozy fabric cubes are a great small-scale storage solution for things like yarns, fabric scraps, patterns, or whatever you collect in your creative space. They are also perfect for playrooms or kids' rooms to store stuffed animals, various tiny toys, or even socks! Unlike baskets, these cubes won't poke or scratch little hands because they're soft and can take a tumble.

Supplies

FABRIC

10 squares of fabric measuring 9" × 9" (5 for inside, 5 for outside)

5 squares of heavy, double-sided fusible interfacing, measuring 8" × 8"

Hand-sewing needle

Yardstick

Fabric scissors or rotary cutter and mat

MY COLOR NOTES

I chose a bold multicolored print to make this storage cube. If you want to store items that will be organized by color, you may choose to represent that with the fabrics. Make your cube snazzy by choosing different fabrics for the inside and the outside.

Cut

1 Cut out ten squares of fabric squared on the grain, measuring precisely 9" × 9". If you want the inside to be different from the outside, cut five squares each out of your two fabrics.

2 Cut five squares of heavy, double-sided fusible interfacing, measuring exactly 8" × 8". Be sure you've chosen very firm almost cardboard-like interfacing.

Prepare the Inner Base

3 Center one square of fusible interfacing on the *wrong* side of one square of inner fabric, hold it in place as you turn it over, and press from the *right* side of the fabric to fuse them together. This will become the inside bottom of your cube; set it aside.

Assemble the Inner Sides

4 Stitch together two pieces of your inner fabric with *right* sides together down one side, with a ½" seam allowance, and backstitching at both ends.

5 Continue to stitch all four pieces together in a row, and join the two end pieces together in the same manner as in Step 4. You should now have what looks like a fabric tube with four seams.

6 With the *right* side wrapped around the narrow end of the ironing board, press open all seams of your tube. This will become the four inner sides of your cube.

7 Repeat Steps 4, 5, and 6 with the four pieces of the outer side fabric. Turn the *right* side out.

Attach Inner Sides to the Base

8 Laying the inner bottom piece down with the *right* side facing up, align the bottom edges of one section of your joined inner sides and one side of your inner bottom piece with the *right* sides together. Making sure that your seams are lining up in each of the inner bottom piece corners, you can start pinning in place all around to join the inner sides to the inner bottom. Let the upper part of the inner sides fold in a bit toward the center of the bottom piece to keep it out of your way as you prepare to stitch around the square.

9 Begin stitching with a ½" seam allowance, starting ½" away from the inner bottom piece edge, which should also be right in the center of one of the seams of the inner sides. Then continue all around, stopping at each corner ½" away from the edge, and turn with the needle down to hold it in place. This will be the bottom seam of the cube.

10 Finish stitching by overlapping the beginning of your stitch, and backstitch. Clip the seam allowance corners off. Set it aside.

Join the Inner and Outer Sides

11 Place the joined outer sides inside the inner sides with the *right* sides together, aligning the upper edges and matching up the four corner seams, and pin in place. Stitch all around with a ½" seam allowance. This will be the top seam of the cube.

12 Reach into the center and pull up the outer sides so that you can lay the double-length cube *right* side against the narrow end of the ironing board, and press open the top seam of the cube all the way around.

13 Now fold the outer top pieces down, and *right* side out, so that the top seam is in line all the way around at the top edge. Press this top edge to crease it. Check to be sure that your outer sides extend down to the same length as the edge of the seam allowance of the inner sides and inner bottom.

Begin to Form the Cube

14 Hooking the fabric cube over the narrow end of the ironing board, insert one of your 8" × 8" fusible interfacing squares in between the outer and inner sides until it fits very snugly into place within the seam lines of one cube side. Also be sure the inner sides you are about to fuse to the interfacing are free from any loose threads. You may need to reach your fingers up inside to the top edge and hold the seam allowance down out of the way, to lay the top edge of the interfacing down flat on top of it. Make sure that you have the interfacing square pressed firmly against the inner top seam, so that there is still ½" of outer-side fabric that extends beyond the interfacing at the bottom.

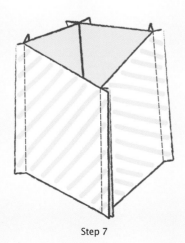

Step 7

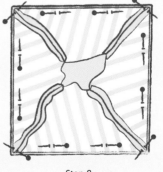

Step 8

15 Once you have the interfacing set into position, press with the iron to fuse the fabric. At the top edge, you may want to press it with downward motions toward the bottom of the cube, so that you are getting the top seam edge pressed really well against the top edge of the interfacing. (Once you have the top edge area fused, you may need to slide a book or thick, wooden block into the bottom inside corners of the cube to provide an appropriate pressing form as you fuse.)

16 Turn the cube over onto the top of the ironing board and press from the inside so that you have fused the inner and outer fabrics on both sides of the interfacing.

17 Repeat Steps 14, 15, and 16 with the remaining three sides of the cube until you have formed your cube. (Because it's a little tricky to reach down into the inner corners of the cube to fuse the inner fabric, you may have to go over a few times with the iron until it's fused well. Be sure to follow the instructions for your particular fusible interfacing.)

Attach the Outer Base

18 Turn the cube on its top and line up the bottom of the outer edges with the seam allowance from the inner edges and inner bottom, and pin together. Hand-sew a long-running basting stitch all the way around, about ¼" from the edge to hold it in place.

19 Fold down this seam allowance on two opposing sides against the bottom of the cube, and press the edges down a bit to help form that 90-degree edge on the bottom perimeter.

20 Repeat Step 19 on the other two sides of the seam allowance, and pin overlapping corners down. Tack those corners in place with a whip stitch to make it as flat as possible against the cube's underside.

21 With the *wrong* side facing up, fold in and press a ½" hem around all edges of the remaining square of fabric. This is the bottom piece of your cube.

22 Center this bottom piece with the *wrong* side against the bottom of the cube, making sure you cover all the raw edges and basting stitches from Steps 17, 18, and 19. Pin in place at the corners and centers of each side. You can also press it against the bottom a little to help keep it in place.

23 Blind-stitch the bottom on, all the way around, making sure to keep all the edges in line with the bottom as well as possible.

24 Finish by giving it a good pressing on the bottom. You may need to hold a small, thick book or wooden block up on the inner side, and press up with one hand for some resistance as you press down with the iron using the other hand.

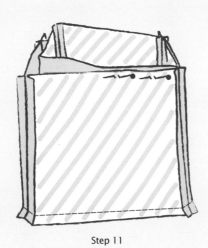

Step 11

Step 18

Pin Cushion Caddy

This little pin cushion will travel with you to the couch, the porch, the bed, or anywhere that your sewing takes you. There's a cubby for your scissors, your thread, and any other hand-sewing essentials for your mobile sewing. You'll be able to find everything, even if you're on a haystack

Supplies

FABRIC

8 scraps at least 4" × 8", 1 piece at least 10" × 12"

Heavy, double-sided fusible interfacing (It should be firm almost cardboard-like.)

Fiberfill

Aluminum foil

Fabric scissors

Craft scissors

Hand-quilting needle

Cardboard or poster board

MY COLOR NOTES

I cut my pin cushion pieces from vintage hand-pieced quilt blocks. The old hand stitching is visible between some of the pieces, but the result is playful and nostalgic.

Cut

1   Cut patterns **1A**, **1B**, **1C**, **1D**, **1E**, **1F** from Pattern Page 1 with craft scissors.

2   Cut eight of pattern piece **1A**, one each from your eight assorted fabrics.

3   Cut one of pattern piece **1B**, a 4½" circle from your larger piece of fabric.

4   Cut one of pattern piece **1C**, a 5" circle from your larger piece of fabric.

5   Cut one of pattern piece **1D**, a 3½" circle from fusible interfacing.

6   Cut one rectangle that measures 11" × 3½" from the fusible interfacing.

7   Cut one of pattern piece **1E**, a 4" circle from cardboard poster board.

8   Cut one of pattern piece **1F** from your larger piece of fabric.

Assemble the "Ball"

9   With two **1A** pieces *right* sides together, sew along one long side from top to bottom at a ³/₈" seam width using the straight-stitch setting. Keep your stitch length on a short stitch setting to help make smooth curves. You'll want to backstitch to knot at the beginning and end of the stitch.

10   Continue Step 9, in the fabric order of your choice, with the rest of the **1A** pieces, adding one after the other to the row of side-by-side pieces until you have a long line of all of them.

11   Press each seam allowance to one side. This curved shaped fits pretty well against the curve on the narrow end of the ironing board.

12 Join the two end **1A** pieces, *right* sides together, stitch from the top down about 1½" in length, and stop with backstitching. Then start your stitching again 1½" away from the bottom, beginning and ending with backstitching. Set aside.

Begin the Inner "Tube"

13 Center the fusible interfacing rectangle to the *wrong* side of piece **1F** and press from the *right* side of the fabric. Follow the directions on your fusible interfacing to get the best adhesion.

14 Stitch the short ends of piece **1F** *right* sides together with a ½" seam allowance and backstitching to knot on both ends. Avoid stitching through the interfacing.

15 Baste the seams open by hand against the interfacing to hold them in place.

Join the "Ball" and Inner "Tube"

16 Turn the fabric "ball" *right* side out and slide it into the tube you've created with the piece **1F** until the edges of each meet at one end. (Smooth them against each other to check if they fit well together. If they don't, you may need to adjust the depths of your seam allowances, as sewn in Step 9, until the ball and the tube have the same circumference.)

17 Baste the edges together by hand just above the line of interfacing, not going through the interfacing. (Basting in a small space like this is easier than pinning.) Then sew carefully on the machine all the way around in the same line. If you find it difficult to machine sew this step, you can make very small, uniform straight stitches instead of basting. Turn the ball *right* side out and down over the tube.

18 Center the fusible interfacing circle (**1D**) onto the *wrong* side of the 4½" fabric circle (**1B**); then press from the *right* side of the fabric to fuse them together.

Close the "Tube"

19 Fit the fused circle into place *right* sides together at the bottom end of the tube, opposite from the end you sewed in Step 18, and pin in place. The edges that extend beyond the interfacings will be the seam allowance. Hand-stitch a short running stitch all the way around, just above the interfacing, to secure the tube bottom in place.

20 Now match those edges with the edges of the bottom of the ball and hand-sew a long basting stitch through all three layers of fabric about ¼" from the edges. Before you knot and finish the thread, gently pull on it to gather the seam allowance up against the bottom of the interfacing circle until it fits snugly. Secure with a few whip stitches and knot.

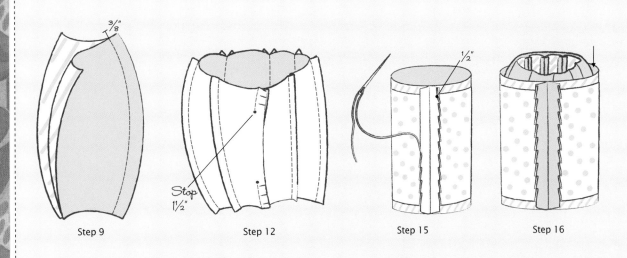

Step 9   Step 12   Step 15   Step 16

Stuff It

21 Taking small amounts of fiberfill at a time, begin stuffing into the side of the ball form in the hole created from Step 14, reaching around each side to get it all stuffed firmly so that it will fill out the whole shape.

22 Blind-stitch (or slip-stitch) the opening closed after the ball is sufficiently stuffed.

Finish the Caddy

23 Using the "Super Circles" technique with the aluminum foil (see page 57 in Chapter 5), press your 5" fabric circle's (**1C**) *wrong* side around the 4" cardboard or poster board (**1E**) to get a smooth, turned edge.

24 Center the pressed circle's *wrong* side against the bottom of the ball, making sure you've covered all the unfinished raw edges. Press just a bit against the fusible interfacing to hold it in place.

25 Blind-stitch the circle onto the form using a small quilting needle.

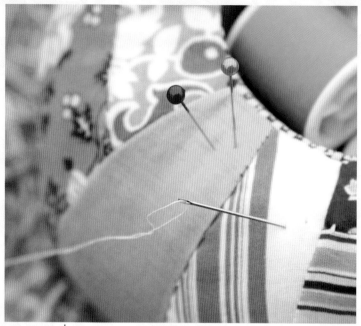

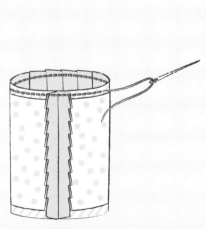

Step 17

Step 18

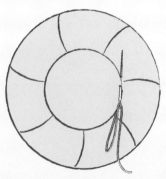

Step 25

Magnetic Personality

The look of this magnet board is only limited by you and your favorite fabric, which is great news! After you've wrapped up this little project, be sure to zip forward to the next project so that you can make some fun magnets to go on your new board. Everyone will admire your attractive homemade goods.

Supplies

FABRIC

2 pieces of light- to medium-weight fabric (at least 2" larger, in width and height, than your foam core)

Thin, flat sheet metal. (The metal has to be magnetic, such as zinc-coated steel or galvanized flashing, which can be found at home improvement stores.)

Tin snips (if you buy the metal sheeting larger than you need)

Foam core (at least 1" larger, in width and height, than your sheet metal)

Craft knife

Duct tape

Fabric scissors

Yardstick

Spray adhesive

Ribbon, about 3 yards

Hand-sewing needle

MY COLOR NOTES

Because this fabric will be the background for the pictures and items you post on it, I went with a smaller and finer print that won't distract too much. I also kept in mind how the fabric would look with black-and-white as well as color photos of loved ones. Everyone looks good in pink! For the ribbons, I chose a complementary color and pattern.

1 When you purchase the metal sheeting, you may want to have some magnets handy to be sure you are getting magnetic metal (aluminum and stainless steel are not). Determine the size you want for your metal board, and the rest of the material measurements will follow this size.

2 Cut your foam core with a craft knife to be longer and wider than your sheet metal by 1" on each side.

3 Spray some adhesive on one side of your metal, and immediately center it on the foam core and press firmly all over. You'll want to do this outside and possibly with a protective mask to avoid inhaling the fumes.

4 Starting at one corner and going toward the opposite corner, layer duct tape over the edge of the metal by no more than a ½" and wrap it around to the back. Press firmly on both sides. Repeat this on all four sides of the board, and set it aside.

5 Measure and cut both your front piece and your back piece of fabric to be 2" longer in each direction than your foam core.

6 Cut six lengths of ribbon at about 18" each.

7 Lay two ribbons side by side at either side of the center point of the fabric top, aligning edges and *right* sides together. Pin them in place and then do the same with the other two pairs of ribbon, an equal distance from the center ribbon, wherever you desire, but at least 2" or 3" from the sides.

8 Sew the ribbons to the fabric with a ½" seam allowance, backstitching over the ribbons at least once to secure them well.

9 Pin together *right* sides of the fabric, letting the ribbons lie in between, and avoid pinning the loose ends anywhere else. Leave either the right or left side of the fabric rectangles open.

10 Sew the top, one side, and bottom together at a ⅝" seam allowance and with a short stitch length.

11 Clip the two corners that are sewn and turn them *right* side out, poking out the corners neatly.

12 Press all the sewn edges with an iron, invert the open end ⅝" inward, and press a crease.

13 Now slide your metal board into the opening with the metal side facing the front piece of fabric.

14 Blind-stitch the opening by hand to close it.

15 Tie the ribbons into bows or knots for hanging. You may need to redo this once you hang it to get it level, and then you can trim your ribbons to a desired length.

Step 4

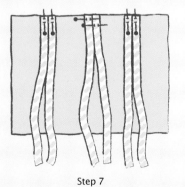

Step 7

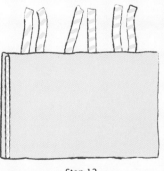

Step 12

1968

Opposites Attract

Whether you've already made the "Magnetic Personality" fabric magnet board or not, this project is a fun and simple way to make some adorable magnets. You'll also learn a charming traditional quilt craft known as the yo-yo. Now that I've gotten the hang of making yo-yo's, it has become a favorite thing to do in front of a good movie.

Supplies

FABRIC

Scraps of fabrics measuring
5" × 7" for each magnet

Cardboard or poster board

Lightweight, double-sided fusible
web (I used Steam-A-Seam)

Hot glue gun

Strong round magnets

Craft scissors

Fabric scissors

Hand-sewing needle

MY COLOR NOTES

This is really a scrap project, but I chose fabrics from my leftover piles that would coordinate with the ribbons and fabric that I used for the "Magnetic Personality" project. The magenta, yellow, and blue pop against the mostly pale pink-and-white fabric background.

Cut

1   Cut patterns **4A** and **4B** from Pattern Page 1 with craft scissors.

2   Cut one of pattern piece **4A**, a 4½" circle, and one from pattern piece **4B**, a 2" circle, from the same fabric.

3   Cut out one 2" circle from cardboard, making sure your edges are smooth.

4   Cut out one 2" circle from fusible web.

Assemble the Inside Form

5   Sandwich the 2" fusible web circle in between the 2" cardboard circle and the 2" fabric circle. Make sure your fabric circle is on top with the *right* side facing up. Press with an iron for just a few seconds to fuse all three layers together.

Make a Yo-Yo

6   Double-thread your needle with an extra-long piece of strong thread. Don't worry about knotting it at all, but do keep it double length all the way to the end. You'll need enough to go all around the circle with several inches to spare.

7 With the *wrong* side of the 4½" fabric circle facing you, fold in the edge about ¼" and start a running stitch (see page 55) very close to the folded edge. Don't pull your thread all the way through, but let plenty of it dangle off at the end.

8 Continue to fold and stitch all the way around, keeping your stitches an equal distance away from each other and very close to the folded edge until you have hand-stitched a hem all the way around without overlapping stitches. You should be left with a circle that is a little pouch-like.

9 Though the edges of the circle will naturally be drawn up, leave them open enough to insert the fabric-covered cardboard into the center of the pouch, cardboard side down.

10 Now take both ends of the thread (one will still have the needle attached), and tug on them like a drawstring to cinch up the center of the "yo-yo." As you do this, you should situate the puckered circle as close to the center of the cardboard circle as possible.

11 Once the center is nice and tight (be careful not to break the thread), clip the thread ends to a length that you can comfortably tie in a knot. Carefully tie the ends together tightly, trying not to loosen up the center gathers at all. Tie a few times to secure it.

12 Tuck the thread ends inside under the yo-yo, using a pencil tip or tweezers.

Add the Magnet

13 Dab a spot of hot glue on the back of the yo-yo and attach to the magnet, pressing firmly to push the glue into the fibers of the fabric and through to the cardboard.

14 Repeat all steps as many times as you wish for a lot of magnets!

Flowery-ish Options

For a magnet that looks a little more like a flower, try out this variation: On your 2" circle of fabric that gets fused to the cardboard and goes on the inside, choose a fabric that contrasts the outer fabric well. For example, if your outer fabric is blue, choose a yellow or orange for the small, inner circle. Also, instead of using a 4½" circle for the outer fabric that becomes a yo-yo, use a smaller one, like a 3½" circle. Follow all the same steps as the regular project. You'll notice, though, that using a smaller outer yo-yo circle will leave more of the center showing from the inside, like a flower. If you wanted to take an extra step toward gardening your magnets, you could attach a little cut felt leaf to the back, next to the magnet, with hot glue.

Step 8

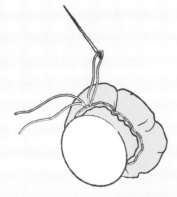

Step 9

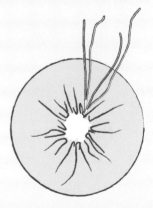

Step 11

Wall Pockets

Though this project is a little involved, it is so worth it! The result is a fabulous, professional-looking set of three wall pockets where you can stash anything from magazines to make-up, depending on where you decide to hang it.

Supplies

FABRIC

> 2 yards for outer fabric
>
> 1 yard for pocket lining

Light- or medium-weight double-sided fusible interfacing

Metal grommets, approximately 1" in diameter

Appropriately sized grommet tool set

Hammer

Cardboard or mat board

Craft knife

Cutting mat

Scissors

Yardstick

MY COLOR NOTES

Since I planned this for a particular room, I took the floral blue walls into consideration. I chose the red outer fabric to be a complement and to act as a frame for the paler, vintage-style print on the inside. The inner fabric print has a hint of the same blues as the walls but is not overly matched.

Cut

1 Cut one pattern piece **5A** from Pattern Page 1 with craft scissors.

2 Cut from outer fabric:
   - Six triangles using the pattern piece **5A**
   - Three pocket backs measuring 13" × 13"
   - Three pocket fronts measuring 13" × 8"
   - Two front panel sections measuring 14" × 13"
   - One bottom front panel section measuring 14" × 16"
   - One top band measuring 14" × 4"
   - One back panel measuring 42" × 14"

Note: Wait until the front is assembled to cut this, as it needs to match the front dimensions perfectly. These dimensions may vary a bit after the front is pieced.

3 Cut from pocket lining fabric:
   - Six triangles using the pattern piece **5A**
   - Three pocket fronts measuring 13" × 8"
   - Three pocket backs measuring 13" × 13"

4 Cut from fusible interfacing
   - One top band lining measuring 13" × 3"

5 Cut from cardboard or mat board
   - Three pieces measuring 6¾" × 11¾"
   - Three pieces measuring 11¾" × 11¾"

Assemble the Pockets

6 With your pocket lining materials, align the narrow point of the pocket triangle sides with the bottom-right corner of the pocket back, with *right* sides together. Stitch the side triangle to the back side with a ½" seam allowance from the top of the side to the bottom of the side, backstitching on both ends. Repeat on the left side.

7 Press open both seams and leave the joined pieces open, *right* side facing up.

8 With the *right* sides together, align the front pocket piece with the pocket side of the joined side and back, and pin in place. You'll have to turn the pocket front a bit to then align it along the bottom and pin it. Finish by pinning up the final side, as well.

9 Begin stitching the front pocket piece to the back and side pocket pieces at the top of the pocket side, and stop ½" away from the bottom with the needle down. (This point should be *right* in the middle of the back and side seam.) Raise the machine foot, turn the pocket, and then lower the foot again so that you can sew across the bottom, stopping ½" away from the other side with the needle down (again, this point should be right in the middle of the back and side seam). Raise the foot again, turn the pocket once more, and then lower the foot to continue the stitch at the top of the pocket side and backstitch to knot.

10 Clip the corners off of the bottom pocket seam allowance, and press open the front corner seams of the pocket. Press the bottom seam up to one side, and set it aside.

11 Repeat Steps 6 through 10 with the remaining two pocket linings and the three outer pockets.

12 Pair up each pocket lining with an outer pocket so that you have three sets. Leave the pocket linings inside out. Turn the outer pockets *right* side out. In each set, fit the outer pocket down inside the pocket lining so that the *right* sides are together.

13 Align both of the upper back sides, the seams, and the pocket front top. Pin along those lines, keeping the front pocket seams open and letting the back pocket seam allowance pin forward. You should have pinned what looks like a bent U-shape.

14 Stitch along that line with a ½" seam allowance, raising and lowering your needle at the back corners to make the 90-degree turn smoothly. Carefully snip the inner corner seam allowance toward the seam corner.

15 Turn out the pockets to the *right* side and fit the lining down into the outer pocket smoothly, poking out the corners and smoothing with your fingers as necessary. Press all the edges well with the iron.

16 Topstitch the edges that you have seamed in Step 14, stitching carefully ⅛" away from the edge. Press again.

17 Slide the smaller cardboard or mat board gently down the opening in the top back until it is firm against the bottom seam. Reach in and pull the pocket lining up, and place it behind the cardboard so that the cardboard is now between the front-pocket lining fabric and the outer pocket fabric. Smooth as necessary.

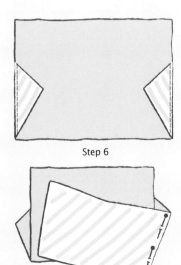

Step 6

Step 8

Step 13

Step 14

18 Now slide the larger square cardboard piece into the top back until it also rests firmly in place along the bottom seam. Tug up on the top back pieces to make sure you have a ½" seam allowance that extends above the cardboard.

Note: If you have not kept your topstitching at ⅛" from the edge consistently, it may be hard to fit in the cardboard.

19 Pin the top pieces together with edges aligned accurately, and machine-baste them together with a ¼" seam allowance. You will need to hold on firmly to this as it goes through the machine because the cardboard is already inserted. It is a little like driving on uneven lanes to have part of your machine's presser foot on the board and not the other half. Just go a little slower than normal, and you'll be fine.

20 Repeat Steps 13 through 19 with the remaining two sets of pocket linings and outer pockets. Set them aside.

Assemble the Back

21 Fuse the interfacing onto the *wrong* side of the top band by centering it within that top band and pressing it from the *right* side of the fabric.

22 With the *right* sides together, pin the 14" side of the top band and the 14" side of one of the front panel sections together. Stitch them together with a ½" seam allowance, but only an inch from the edge on both sides, leaving most of the seam open.

23 In the same manner, attach the other front panel section to the bottom of the first front panel section, with only 1" of stitching at each end.

24 Again, do the same with the larger bottom-front panel section so that they are all joined. Press all the seam allowances toward the top band.

25 If you haven't cut the back panel piece, do so now and be sure it measures to the exact dimensions of the joined front panel pieces. It's fine if it doesn't match the length specified above exactly. What does matter is that the front and back panels are the same size.

26 With the *right* sides together, pin and sew the front and back panels together all the way around with a ½" seam allowance, overlapping your beginning stitches with a backstitch. Be sure that you are allowing the seams of the front panels to stay pressed up as you sew.

27 Clip the corners off and turn it *right* side out through any one of the openings, poking out the corners neatly. Lay it out flat, and press all the edges well. It might be helpful to keep the front pinned to the back in a few spots to keep the large openings from gaping as you are working with the piece.

28 Topstitch the entire perimeter of the panels over the last seam you made, staying ⅛" away from the edge.

29 Starting with the bottom pocket, slide the pocket top into the opening between the bottom front panel and the middle front panel until you have ½" of the pocket top concealed, and centered within the panel. Pin through all layers of fabric.

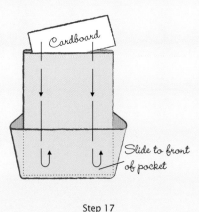

Cardboard

Slide to front of pocket

Step 17

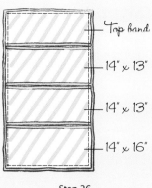

Top band

14" x 13"

14" x 13"

14" x 16"

Step 26

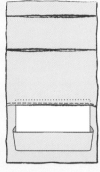

Step 30

Assemble the Wall Pocket

30 Topstitch along this line from edge to edge, backstitching at both ends. Again, employ the same care as in Step 14 regarding the cardboard lining. You may need to roll up the top end of the panels to keep them out of your way as you sew.

31 Continue Steps 28 and 29 with the middle pocket and then the top pocket, until all are joined together.

Finish with the Grommets

32 After you've pressed both sides of the top band well to fuse the interfacing, find the two level points in the top band where you would like to set your grommets, and mark the centers with a marker point. This will get cut out, and so it doesn't have to be a soluble marker.

33 With a fine-point pen or pencil, trace the circle where the grommet will go using the grommet piece. Using a craft knife, cut some lines similar to an asterisk within the circle.

34 Then begin carefully cutting away all the fabric inside the circle, one pie-shape at a time. You should then be able to easily insert the eyelet from underneath and through the hole.

35 Place the top piece on and use the tool and hammer to pound both pieces together. Refer to the specific package directions with the particular grommet and grommet tool that you have.

The Great Dress Escape

For those serendipitous occasions where you can manage yourself and just a few dresses out of the house for a day or two, whether for business or for kicks, this garment bag proves a faithful companion. Without the complication of crazy-pocketed luggage suitable for a two-month stay on the edge of the world, this simple dress bag paired with your favorite overnight bag is the perfect answer to traveling light. It also serves as a safe spot in the closet for your fanciest of frocks to hang out when the only place you have to be is home.

Supplies

FABRIC

1¾ yards of 54" fabric

or

3½ yards of 44" fabric

For trim fabric:

4½ yards of bias strips

⅓ yard fabric for the bottom band

2 1½" × 52" strips

Medium-weight interfacing

1 zipper at least 54" long (zipper by the yard is great)

1 large curtain grommet

Pencil or marker

Yardstick

Fabric scissors or rotary cutter and mat

MY COLOR NOTES

I chose an oilcloth to make this bag because it is durable and waterproof. The slick surface eases moving garments in and out of the bag. Using a nice, durable home-décor fabric would be perfectly suitable, as well. This black-and-white print seemed like a decadent, yet timeless, design that would take me on a lot of trips in style. Trimming it out with a bright cotton print finishes it off with just the right dose of surprise.

Cut

1   Cut two rectangles measuring 24" wide and 48" long. These are the bag front and bag back.

2   Cut two strips of fabric that are 1½" wide and 48" long. This is the zipper trim.

3   Cut two rectangles measuring 5" wide and 25" long for the bottom band.

4   Cut one rectangle from medium-weight interfacing, measuring 4½" wide and 25" long.

5   Cut and join as many 2" wide bias strips together as necessary to make about 4½ yards of bias. Refer to the "Maybe I'm Bias" tutorial in Chapter 4 for tips on cutting and joining bias strips.

6   With one of the rectangles that you cut in Step 1, fold it in half lengthwise. Make a mark at the top edge, 1" away from the fold. Make another mark on the side edges that is 2" away from the top edge. Draw an angled line between these marks.

7   Cut through both layers of the folded piece on this angled line.

8   On the top edge and starting a few inches away from the side edge, redraw the outer corner to be a little more curved instead of a sharp turn. Now cut on this curved line.

9 Now use the new shape of this rectangle as a pattern to cut the other rectangle identically by laying the new one over the previous rectangle and cutting. These are the front piece and back piece for the garment bag.

10 Cut two small facings from the trim fabric that are only 2" wide and are the same shape as the center tops.

Attach the Zipper

11 Fold the front piece (which could be either, since they're the same) in half lengthwise again, *wrong* sides together. Make a few marks on the outer edge of the fold all along the length. Then open the fold and draw a straight line on the *right* side using a straightedge, connecting those dots down the center from the top to the bottom. (This can be done with a regular pencil or marker, because it will get cut off later.) This will be the bag front.

12 With the back of the zipper against the *right* side of the bag front, place the zipper center along the centerline that you drew in Step 11, letting a few inches and the zipper head hang beyond the top center point of the bag front. Pin it in place.

13 With the zipper trim strips, press back ½" toward the *wrong* side along one long edge of each of the strips.

14 With the *right* sides together, lay the zipper trim on top of the zipper, lining up the unfolded edge of the trim with the outside edge of the zipper. Transfer the pins from the zipper to include pinning through the trim, the zipper, and the bag front.

15 Sew all three layers together using a zipper foot, about ¼" away from the outer zipper edge.

16 Repeat Steps 13 and 14 on the other side of the zipper with the remaining zipper trim piece.

17 Turn the zipper trims out away from the zipper, folding them back on their seam line, and topstitch their outside folded edges down, all along the length of the zipper. Press. (If you are using oilcloth, place a piece of cloth over it while you press to keep the iron from scorching (or burning) the oilcloth.

18 Slide the zipper head down a few inches below the top edge of the front. Sew on the top facing, with the *right* side of the facing against the *wrong* side of the bag front, across the top only from edge to edge, with a ½" seam allowance.

19 Turn the facing toward the *right* side of the bag front, letting the seam lie in the top edge of the fold. Fold the bottom edge of the facing inward toward its *wrong* side and under the seam allowance, and topstitch all layers down close to the bottom folded edge of the facing.

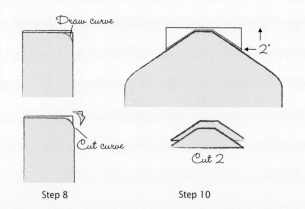

Draw curve

Cut curve

Cut 2

Step 8   Step 10

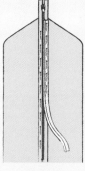

Step 14

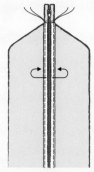

Step 17

20 On the *wrong* side of the front, carefully poke the bottom blade of your scissors just below the horizontal stitch line that you made in Step 17 and in between the zipper seams from Steps 15 and 16, pointing toward the bottom of the front. Once you get your bottom blade inserted between the front piece and the zipper, cut the front piece all the way down the center, staying precisely between the zipper seams.

21 Now cut away most of this seam allowance close to the zipper seams on both sides.

Assemble the Garment Bag

22 Apply the *right* side of the remaining facing to the *wrong* side of the back piece at the top, and stitch across with a ½" seam allowance. Turn the facing toward the *right* side, folding the bottom edge of the facing underneath the seam allowance, and topstitch the same way you've done in Step 19 on the front piece.

23 With the *wrong* sides together, sew the front to the back from the top edge, around the outer curve and down the side with a ½" seam allowance. Repeat on the opposite side.

24 Press the long edge of the bias ½" toward the *wrong* side.

25 Fold back the end of the bias ½" toward *wrong* side and press.

26 With the *right* sides together and starting at the top center-right of the front and the top folded end of the bias, align the unfolded long edge of the bias with the edge of the bag and sew them together from the top, around the outer curve and down to the bottom with a ½" seam allowance, directly over the stitching from Step 23. Be sure to stretch the bias just slightly as you sew it around the outer curve. Trim off excess bias.

27 Now wrap the folded edge of the bias around to the back, and line it up along the stitch lines to barely just cover them. Do this as you topstitch it in place from top to bottom, very close to the folded edge of the bias, also being sure that the topstitching stays in line inside the bias on the other side.

28 Repeat Steps 22 and 23 on the other side with the remaining bias. Press the trim on both sides. (Be careful to press only the trim and not the oilcloth if you're using oilcloth.)

29 Lay the interfacing on top of the *wrong* side of one of the bottom band pieces, aligning three of their sides together. Sew them together with a ³/₈" seam allowance on only the two short ends.

30 With the *right* sides together, sew the bottom band pieces together on only their short ends with a ½" seam allowance.

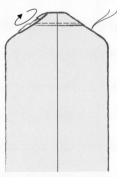

Step 19

Step 20

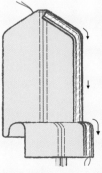

Step 26

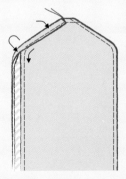

Step 27

31 Slide the bottom edges of the bag in between the *right* sides of the bottom band until all bottom edges match up. Pin them in place. Be sure that the side of the bottom band that has the interfacing lined up against its edge is the edge that you've aligned the bottom of the bag with.

32 Across the bottom edge, sew through all layers (which might require a heavy-duty machine needle, like a size 16) with a ½" seam allowance.

33 Turn the bottom band to their *right* sides and press (a). Fold up both of the bottom edges of the bottom band inward toward the *wrong* side ½" and around the edge of the interfacing (b), and pin them in place (c).

34 Topstitch around the entire perimeter of the bottom band. Press.

35 Install a large grommet in the very center of the bottom band using the directions that came with the grommet.

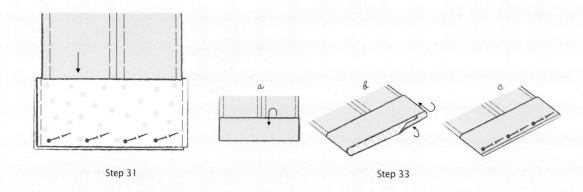

Step 31

Step 33

Chapter 7

Stylize

I'll Have One of Everything Bag

Why force yourself into deciding which fabric to use when you can have a little of everything with this multi-panel bag. Echoing the "circular blades" of the Dresden Plate quilt, this bag uses your favorite fabric scraps. It's also an ideal size for everyday use as you're out in the world conquering life's really difficult decisions, like which breakfast pastry to choose.

Supplies

FABRIC

- 8 assorted cotton fabrics, less than ¼ yard each
- ½ yard for lining
- 12 assorted strips of fabric, 2" x 40"

Medium-weight interfacing

Craft scissors

Fabric scissors or rotary cutter and mat

Hand-sewing needle

MY COLOR NOTES

I chose all my fabrics for this bag with a neutral/red/black scheme in mind, and just continued layering one next to another until I found the right mix. All the prints are fine-handed (or hand drawn) with a lot of sketch-like qualities that keep the look of the bag unified.

Cut

The cutting for this bag needs to be very accurate so that the outer side of the purse will line up well with the lining. For Steps 1 through 4, you'll need to cut each of the pattern pieces from two different fabrics if you want to have a total of eight different fabric panels on each side.

1 Cut patterns **8A**, **8C**, **8D**, and **8E** from Pattern Page 2, and **8B** from Pattern Page 3, with craft scissors.

2 Cut two *right* sides together from pattern **8B** for the front side. Repeat for the back side.

3 Cut two *right* sides together from pattern **8C** for the front side. Repeat for the back side.

4 Cut two *right* sides together from pattern **8D** for the front side. Repeat for the back side.

5 Cut two *right* sides together from pattern **8E** for the front side. Repeat for the back side.

6 Cut two from pattern **8A** on the fold for the purse lining.

7 Cut two from pattern piece **8A** on the fold from interfacing.

8 Cut two 9" x 4" rectangles on the bias for the strap channels.

Assemble the Bag

Be sure to accurately join all the panels with a ½" seam allowance to ensure a proper fit between the outer bag and the lining.

9 Piece together the front side of the purse using the following sequence. Begin by sewing piece **8B** to piece **8C** with *right* sides together and with a ½" seam allowance. Then sew **8D** to **8C**, and then sew **8E** to **8D** in the same manner.

10 Repeat Step 9 with opposite-facing **8B**, **8C**, **8D**, and **8E** pieces. Then join the two **8B** pieces together in the center to complete the piecing for the purse front. Press all seams open.

11 Repeat Steps 9 and 10 with the back side pieces.

12 Machine-baste one piece of interfacing (**8A**) to the *wrong* side of the paneled front ³/₈" from the edges all the way around. Repeat with the other piece of interfacing on the *wrong* side of the paneled back. (If your pieced front or back is not the same size as your interfacing, perhaps the panels were cut or sewn slightly less than accurately. Adjust any panel seams as necessary to make the paneled front and back the same size as the interfacing.)

13 Press in both short ends of the strap channels ½" toward the *wrong* side of the fabric, and stitch down with a ¼" seam allowance. Repeat on the other strap channel.

14 Fold one of the strap channels in half lengthwise with *wrong* sides together, and align its two unfinished edges with the upper edge of the *right* side of the purse front. Center it between the purse top edge ends, which should leave about ½" of top edge excess on either side of the strap channel. Pin it in place. Repeat with the other strap channel on the back side.

15 Sew the strap channel in place with a ½" seam allowance. Clip the seam allowance. Repeat on the back side.

16 Now pin the *right* sides of the bag front and the bag back together and sew between the stop points (as noted on the lining pattern and pattern **8E**) with a ½" seam allowance, beginning and ending with a backstitch. Leave the needle down ½" away from the corner edge, and lift the presser foot to turn the corners, and continue sewing.

17 Clip the corners, and wedge clip (see Chapter 4) the curved seam allowance. Trim just the interfacing seam allowance to about ¼", but end trimming just below the stopping points. Turn the bag *right* side out. Run your fingers along the inside of the seams to press them out, and then press well with the iron.

18 Sew the lining pieces with right sides together and a ½" seam allowance beginning at stop/start point. Leave the needle down ½" away from the corner edge, and lift the presser foot to turn the first corner. Continue sewing until you've come to an opening point. Begin your sewing again at the other opening point, and continue around the next corner and up to the other stop/start point.

19 Clip the corners.

20 Put the outer bag inside the bag lining so that their *right* sides are together.

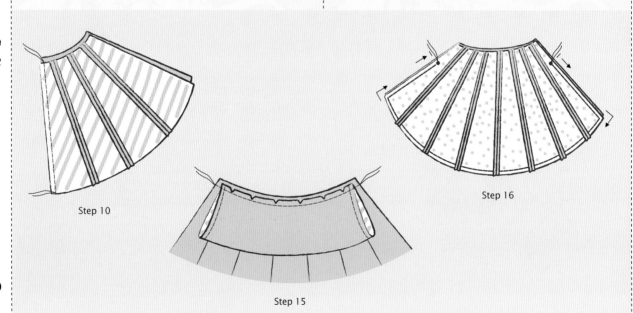

Step 10

Step 15

Step 16

21 Match up the seams at the sides and pin in place on just one side between the points where you stopped sewing the side seams. You'll need to turn the side seam allowances away toward the other side of the bag to reveal the side seam stitching.

22 Now sew up one side, across the top and down the other side with a ½" seam allowance, and do not go through any of the side seam allowances. You should be making your turns at the top corners right beside where the edges of your strap channel are sewn in. Be sure to backstitch at the beginning and end of your stitching, and turn the corners by keeping the needle down and raising the presser foot.

23 Repeat Steps 21 and 22 on the other side of the bag. Clip off the seam allowances at the corners and snip the allowances at the side seams.

24 Reach through the opening you left in the lining's bottom seam and pull the *right* side of the purse *right* side out.

25 Whip stitch the lining's opening closed.

26 Turn the lining back into the inside of the bag. Work with the material until you get all the seams pressed into place with your fingers, and then press well with the iron.

Make the Braided Straps

27 To make the braided straps, you'll want to rip six strips of fabric that are about 2" wide and 36" long for each strap, for a total of 12 strips. The raw edges are a desirable texture for this strap.

28 Safety-pin the ends of six strips together, and pin them closed on the corner of a mattress or some other secure spot. Divide them into three sets of two strips and begin braiding them pretty snugly.

29 Once you reach the ends, trim the strips if they're uneven, and safety-pin the ends together. At the other end, remove the safety pin from the bed and just keep it pinned through the strips.

30 Feed one end of the braided strips through one of the strap channels until you've pulled it through a few inches.

31 Now just with two strips at a time, join the ends of the three sets to themselves and pin them. Either machine-sew a few times across the strips or make a few rows of whip stitches to completely join the ends of the strips together. (It doesn't have to be pretty.)

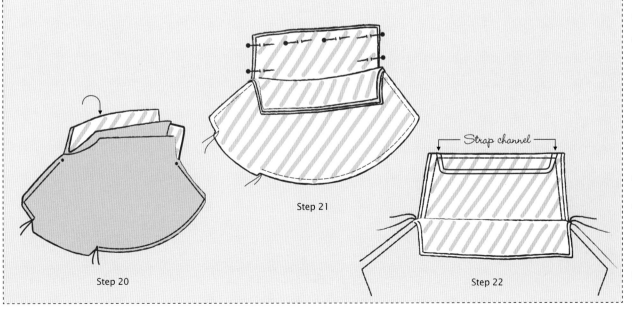

Step 20

Step 21

Strap channel

Step 22

32 Slip the joined part of the braided straps back through the channel to cover up the seams. You can make a few whip stitches on the inside of the strap channel to keep the straps in place. Repeat from Step 28 for the other strap.

Note: To make the bag have some extra dimension at the outer corners, you can use a few extra ripped strips of fabric to make a "grocery bag" style turn down.

33 Press out the outer corner of the bag in the opposite way that it lays naturally so that the side seam and the bottom seam are pressed against each other and forming a triangular point. Fold the center of a few strips over this point and sew them in place, with a few straight stitches on the machine, going across the side seam.

34 Now fold the center of a few more ripped strips of fabric against the bottom edge of the bag on the seam between pieces **8E** and **8D**, and sew in place along the bottom edge with a few straight stitches.

35 You can now tie together the strips from Steps 33 and 34 together into a knot to cinch down the corner of the bag, and make a boxy corner. Trim the length of the strips as desired.

36 Repeat Steps 33, 34, and 35 on the other side.

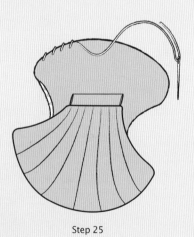

Step 25

Step 28

Step 31

Right Off the Cuff

I had so much fun making these little cuffs that I didn't want to stop! They can be as simple or as embellished as you like. A solid, neutral linen cuff with white vintage buttons could serve as a light and airy summer bracelet. Adding ruffles on one or more edges, playing with assorted mismatched prints, or adding some embroidery are all clever ways to customize this little ditty.

Supplies

FABRIC

⅛ yard or less for each front and back sides

⅛ yard for ruffles (optional)

Buttons

Hand-sewing needle

Tape measure

Fabric scissors or rotary cutter and mat (I recommended using the latter)

Any desired trims

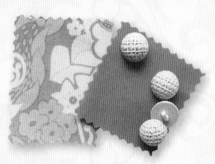

MY COLOR NOTES

For the cuff shown in the previous picture, I chose fabrics to play up the vintage buttons. Your choices may depend on whether you have a certain outfit in mind to wear it with, or if you want one that you can wear with anything. Do consider how any color looks against your skin when choosing fabrics.

Measure and Cut

You'll base the size of your fabric pieces on your wrist measurements and your desired length for the cuff. The cuff in the photo has a finished length of 4".

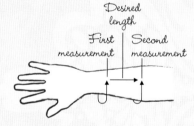

Steps 1, 2, and 3

1 Measure the circumference of your wrist with a tape measure just above your wrist bone; add 1" and write the result here _____.

2 Determine the length you want the cuff to be, add 1", and write the result here _____.

3 Now farther up on your forearm, take another circumference measurement. The distance between the two circumference measurements that you take should equal the finished length you'd like the cuff to be. Add 1" to this circumference measurement and write the result here _____.

4 Fold fabric for the front side of the cuff in half, and then make a perpendicular cut going away from the fold. Then measure from that cut, along the fold line, at a distance equal to your desired cuff length result from Step 2. Make another cut at that mark parallel to the first cut.

5 Now that you have two nice straight edges, you'll need to mark the folded fabric to cut the width of the cuff. Starting at the top edge, make a mark that is a distance from the fold equal to half of your result from Step 1. At the bottom edge, make a mark that is a distance from the fold equal to half your result from Step 3.

6 Connect the marks from Step 5 with a straightedge, and cut an angled line with your rotary cutter.

7 Open this piece and use it as a pattern to cut a second piece for the back side of the cuff.

Note: Skip to Step 13 if you are not making a ruffle.

8 If you want to put ruffles at the top or bottom edge of the cuff, cut 2" wide strips of fabric that are twice the length of your cuff circumference plus about 2". Repeat if you want to have ruffles on both edges.

Begin Sewing

9 With the *wrong* sides together, fold in ½" of the ends of your ruffle, and press.

10 Now fold the strip lengthwise, *wrong* sides together, so that the edges meet, and machine-baste along the entire length ¼" away from the two unfinished edges.

11 Now gather this edge until the length has been reduced to the length of your cuff edge, less 1". Repeat with the remaining second strip if you are making two ruffles. Be sure to read the section, "A Small Gathering," in Chapter 4 for tips on making ruffled gathers.

12 Lay the unfinished edges of the ruffle on the *right* side of the cuff along the top edge, leaving ½" of the cuff on each end. Pin in place and machine-baste with a ³/₈" seam allowance. (Repeat at the opposite edge of the cuff if you'd like to add ruffles to both edges.)

13 Now with the *right* sides together, layer the cuff back on top of the cuff front, thereby sandwiching the ruffles between them (if you have included ruffles). Pin and sew together with a ½" seam allowance on three sides, leaving one of the sides open.

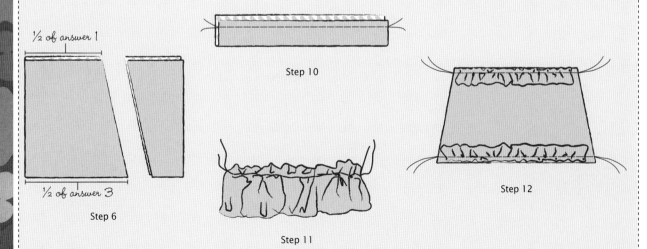

½ of answer 1

½ of answer 3

Step 6

Step 10

Step 11

Step 12

14 Clip the corners of the seam allowance and trim the opposite ends at an angle down toward the opening. Turn the *right* side out and press.

15 Open the side opening, press the seam allowances open with your finger, and then fold in ½" of the side opening edge. Repeat on the other seam. Press so that you have a smooth fold in, and then pin in place.

16 Now topstitch the entire perimeter of the cuff ⅛" from the edge.

17 Determine which side of the cuff you want to face outward, and which wrist you're likely to wear it on. Wrap it around your wrist with the opening of the cuff on the outside of your wrist. The edge that is folding over the top of your wrist will get the button loops, and the edge coming from the underside of your wrist will get the buttons.

18 Sew on as many buttons as you wish within the edge of the cuff's *right* side.

19 You can now follow the "Loop-de-Loop" tutorial in Chapter 5 to make threaded button loops for the buttons. (If you'd rather use small loops of elastic in the edge as button loops, you would need to insert them at Step 13, facing inward in the side seam between the *right* sides of the cuff front, before you sew.)

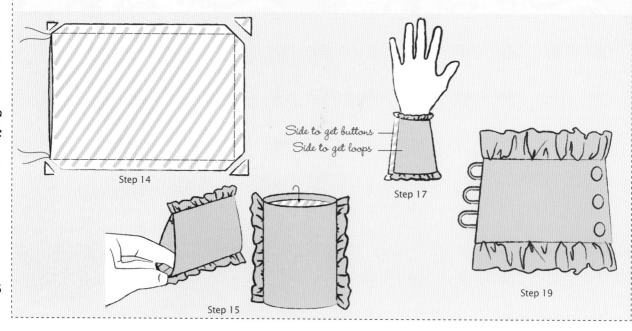

Step 14

Side to get buttons
Side to get loops

Step 17

Step 15

Step 19

Taxi Tote

I have no better excuse for the title of this purse other than that I hate attempting to smoothly swish in and out of taxis as I conduct business in New York City, or any other big city, while lugging complicated, dangling, strap-y things off my shoulder. The design and construction of this bag is so simple that you can slip in and out of anywhere without any fuss. That puts the Taxi Tote high on the function and fashion charts. All hail the Taxi Tote!

Supplies

FABRIC

- ¾ yard for outer purse
- ¾ yard for purse lining
- 1 yard fabric for bias strips and pocket
- Scrap fabric for button cover and button loop

Large-size metal button

Heavyweight interfacing

Craft scissors

Fabric scissors or rotary cutter and mat

Tailor's chalk (optional)

MY COLOR NOTES

In thinking of standing on a street corner hailing a cab, I thought about this bright and eye-catching print. The intensely colored and oversized print paired with this very simple shape makes for a bold statement.

Cut

1   Cut pattern **9A**, which is separated into two parts, from Pattern Page 3 with craft scissors. Tape the sections together, as instructed on the pattern.

2   Cut two purse pieces from the outer fabric on the fold using pattern **9A**, marking the bottom corner points on the pattern with a chalk line or a snip.

3   Cut two lining pieces from the lining fabric on the fold using pattern **9A**, marking the bottom corner points on the pattern with a chalk line or a snip.

4   Cut two interfacing pieces using pattern **9A**.

5   Cut one rectangle from the pocket fabric, measuring 8" x 9".

6   Cut several bias strips that are 2" wide and that will be about 3 yards in length when sewn together.

7   Cut one button loop piece 1" wide and as long as you'll need for your particular button size. Make the length of the button loop twice as long as the diameter of your button plus 2".

8   Cut a fabric circle for the button cover in a size listed on its packaging.

Make Pocket and Trim

9   Turn the pocket top edge ¼" toward the *wrong* side and press. Turn it down ¼" again and topstitch ⅛" away from the edge.

10   Press in the remaining edges ¼" as in Step 9 and pin them in place.

11 Lay the *wrong* side of the pocket on the *right* side of one of the lining pieces in your desired position, and transfer pins to include pinning through the lining piece, as well.

12 Topstitch the pocket in place ⅛" away from the outer edge of the pocket on the sides and bottom. Backstitch at the beginning and end. You can make pocket dividers by making additional vertical seams in the pocket. For example, you can make a narrow one for a pen or a wider one for your cell phone.

13 Join several bias strips together to make a length of bias that is about 3 yards long. Refer to the "Maybe I'm Bias" tutorial in Chapter 4 for tips on cutting and joining bias strips.

14 Press in both long edges of the bias strip ½" toward the *wrong* side so that they meet. Also fold them again in half lengthwise, and press a crease along the center fold. Trim both ends bluntly.

Assemble the Purse

15 At the side and bottom corner points, sew a short line of basting stitches, starting at the edge of the outer purse and down. Do this on both sides of both of the outer pieces and on both sides of both of the lining pieces.

16 Machine-baste the interfacing pieces to the *wrong* sides of the outer purse pieces with a ¼" seam allowance all the way around the perimeter, except for the top edges of the strap. Complete this step with both purse outer pieces and interfacings.

17 Press the 1" button loop strip toward the *wrong* side ½" on each long edge so that the edges meet in the center. Press another crease on the center line where the edges meet to enclose the raw edges. Topstitch down the middle of the button loop. Press.

18 Find the center point of the purse piece that you want to be the back by folding it in half, and mark it with a pin vertically. Place the two ends of the button loop right next to each other on either side of the pin, and pin them in place.

19 Run a few rows of stitching back and forth over the button loops ⅜" way from the top edge.

20 With the *right* sides together, sew the purse outer pieces together, down one side, across the bottom, and up the other side with a ½" seam allowance, leaving the needle down ½" away from the edge at the corners, lifting the presser foot to turn the fabric, and then lowering the presser foot to continue sewing the next side. Backstitch at the beginning and end. Press the seams open.

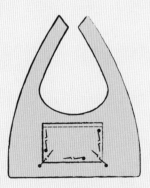

Step 11

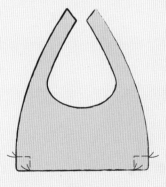

Step 15

Step 16

Chapter 7: **Stylize:** Taxi Tote ∎

Chapter 7: **Stylize:** Taxi Tote ∎

21 With the *right* sides together, and keeping the seam allowances open, sew the center top edges of the strap together with a ½" seam allowance. Trim the interfacing only very close to the stitch line. Press this seam open.

22 At the corners of the purse, where you see the basting stitches from Step 15, open out the front and back sides of the purse from each other, and press the corner out to create a triangular-shaped fold with the corner of the purse as the top point of the triangle. When you do this, make sure that the seams of the side and bottom are pressed against each other and in line with each other. Pin this corner along the basting lines that you made in Step 15.

23 Make a seam across this line of basting stitches, and backstitch at the beginning and end. Trim the corner off.

24 Repeat Steps 22 and 23 on the opposite corner. Turn the purse *right* side out.

25 Repeat Steps 15 through 23 with the purse lining, but do not turn the lining *right* side out.

26 Place the purse lining inside the outer purse so that the *wrong* sides are together. Also be sure to place the pocket side of the lining against the outer side that has the button loop. Pin all of the edges, lining up the top strap seams of the lining and outer purse.

27 Machine-baste all the way around the openings of the bag on both sides, ³/₈" from the edges.

28 Starting just shy of the center, lay the *wrong* side of the inner crease of the bias strip against the edges of the purse top, letting the two folded edges of the bias come down on either side of the purse to sandwich the purse in between. Pin them in place, through all layers.

29 Begin sewing through all layers down the center of the bias strip from the *right* side to attach the bias to the edges. You'll want to move pretty slowly, gently stretching the bias a bit as you sew, to form it smoothly around the curved edges of the bag opening. Also be sure as you go that you are catching the bias on the inner side, by continuing to keep the purse edges in the crease of the bias.

Note: The manner in which the above step is performed, in my opinion, is easier to achieve without pinning the entire bias on first, because you need to allow the bias to "give" some as you move around the opening.

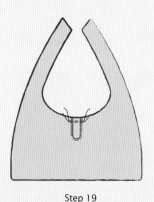

Step 19

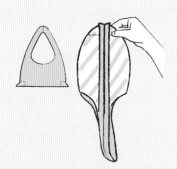

Step 22

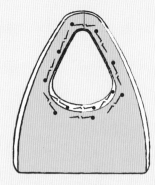

Step 26

Chapter 7: **Stylize:** Taxi Tote

100

30 When you are about 2" or 3" away from where you began in Step 29, put your needle down through the layers (a), and estimate how much bias it will take you to overlap the beginning point, adding a little to fold back the bias toward the *wrong* side of itself at the end. Trim the bias at this estimated point, fold back about ½" toward its *wrong* side (b), replace the crease of the bias back against the top edge of the purse overlapping the other end of the bias, and continue sewing until you've joined the beginning stitches and backstitch (c).

31 Repeat Steps 26 through 30 on the other opening of the purse. Press all edges.

32 Sew the button in place on the front side of the bag, so that the edge of the button is just below the edge of the center front.

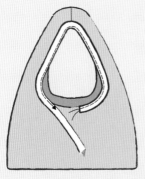

Step 29

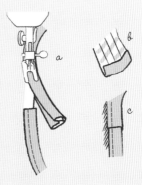

Step 30

Smashing Smock

This smock is so comfy and easygoing that you will reach for it on a daily basis, so make more than one. The beauty of a pattern this classic is that, with a simple change in fabric or length, you could either have a casual blouse to wear alone or over skinny tees, or you could have a charming little dress perfectly suitable for a night out. One pocket, two pockets, small pockets, no pockets. Totally up to you, my friend. And I dare say, you are smashing!

Supplies

FABRIC

- 1/3 yard for yoke
- 1/3 yard for yoke facing
- 2/3 yard for body (more if you want to make into a dress)

Craft paper

Marker

Yardstick

Craft scissors

Fabric scissors or rotary cutter and mat

One button

MY COLOR NOTES

I'm absolutely smitten with this yoke fabric (top pieces); I had to find a way to use it and make it sing. I decided to keep the deep neutral palette by choosing a more subtle black print with sweet little bouquets floating here and there. The pockets are barely there, and only given away by just a thin trim line of a pale calico at their top edge. The result is feminine and nostalgic, but the clean lines of the dark tones keep it modern and striking.

Modify the Pattern's Size

The pattern provided is generally a medium size, and without too much trouble, it can be modified to be smaller or larger. The following is a series of tips to modify the pattern size, and the corresponding illustrations help explain the process.

Determine the Length

The recommended total length for pattern piece **10C** is 19" for a medium, 18" for a small, and 20" for a large. Your height and whether or not you want this to be a dress will determine your final length. Add length by way of extra craft paper and some tape, as shown below.

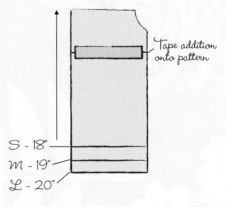

Tape addition onto pattern

S - 18"
m - 19"
L - 20"

For a Larger Size

(a) To make the neck opening slightly larger, as well as increase the width of the yoke, place the fold line edges of pieces **10A** and **10B** a small distance away from the fold of the fabric when you cut. The distance between the pattern and the fold of the fabric needs to be the same for both pieces **10A** and **10B**.

(b) To make the yoke wider, but leave the neck opening the same, cut pattern pieces **10A** and **10B** on the vertical "modify line" line, and put lengths of tape or additional paper between the pieces, connecting them, to increase the size.

(c) To make the body of the smock wider, after you've taped the two sections of **10C** together, simply place the fold line of pattern piece **10C** a small distance away from the fold of the fabric for the front and back pieces (just the front piece if you're expecting!). Don't forget that if you widen the yoke (**10A** and **10B**), you'll also need to widen the body by the same amount.

(d) To make the armholes lower, add 1" or so on the top of pattern piece **10C** for the front and back.

For a Smaller Size

(a) If your shoulders are narrower and you want to decrease the width of the yoke, fold the pattern along the vertical "modify line" on pattern pieces **10A** and **10B**. I suggest folding pattern piece **10A** on the line and just pinning a tuck of it at the top, bottom, and middle. Hold it up against yourself with the center line in the center of your chest to check and readjust if necessary. Then pin pattern piece **10B** by the same amount.

(b) If you want the body of the smock to be narrower, after you've taped the two sections of **10C** together, simply fold in the center fold line edge of pattern **10C** on both the front piece and back piece to make them the same. Open it back up, however, after you've cut the fabric to mark the gathering points.

(c) If you want the yoke to be shorter, and thus raise the armholes a bit, fold the yoke along the horizontal "modify line" on pattern pieces **10A** and **10B**.

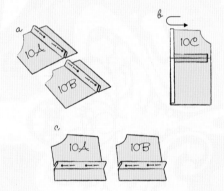

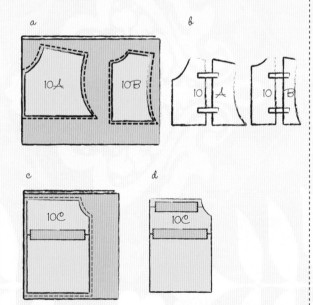

Cut

1 Using craft scissors, cut pattern pieces **10A**, **10B**, and **10C** from Pattern Page 4, and **10C** (continuation) from Pattern Page 5.

2 Cut one of pattern piece **10A** on the fold for the yoke front.

3 Cut one of pattern piece **10A** on the fold for the yoke front facing.

4 Cut two of pattern piece **10B**, opposite, for the yoke backs.

5 Cut two of pattern piece **10B**, opposite, for the yoke back facings.

6 Cut two of pattern piece **10C** on the fold, one for the body front and one for the body back. Make note of the gathering points with pins, nips, or chalk lines.

Note: Pattern piece **10C** is divided into two sections, which should be taped together before you use it to cut the fabric.

7 Cut two lengths of bias strips that are 1½" wide and roughly 10" long. You'll want this to be the same fabric as the smock body fabric. It will become the seam binding for the lower armhole.

8 Cut a 1" strip of fabric for your button loop. Make the strip twice as long as the diameter of your button, plus an extra 1¼". So a ½" button would need a loop that is 2¼" long.

Sew the Yoke

9 With the *right* sides together, sew the shoulder seams of the yoke front to the yoke backs with a ⁵/₈" seam allowance. Press both seams open.

10 Press the long sides of the button loop in toward the *wrong* side until they meet in the center, and then fold again on the center line and press to crease. Topstitch the loop's folds together down the center.

11 On the *right* side of the yoke back, align both ends of the button loop with the center edge of the *right* side of the back. Do this ⁵/₈" away from the top edge. Make sure the button loops are snug next to each other. Run a few machine stitches over them ½" from the center edge to tack them in place.

12 With the *right* sides together, sew the shoulder seams of the yoke front facing to the yoke back facings with a ⁵/₈" seam allowance. Press both seams open.

13 With the *right* sides together, lay the yoke facing over the yoke, matching up all the edges. Pin along the outer arm edges and around the neckline and center back. Sew the arm opening on one side with a ⁵/₈" seam allowance, beginning and ending ⁵/₈" away from the bottom edges of the yoke. Repeat on the other arm opening.

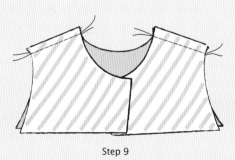

Step 9

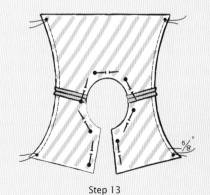

Step 13

14 Now sew the neckline opening and center back of the yoke together in a continuous stitch line with a $5/8$" seam allowance, beginning and ending $1\frac{1}{2}$" away from the bottom edges of the yoke backs. Keep the needle down and raise the presser foot to turn at the center back and neckline corners. Keep a smooth, careful seam allowance along the curved edge of the neck. It's best to have a short stitch length here.

15 Clip the seam allowance corners off of the center top of the back yokes, and nip several places in the curved seam allowance of the neckline. Turn the *right* side out by inverting the yoke backs within each of themselves and pulling them through the front of the yoke. Press inside the seam allowances with your fingers to poke out all the corners and edges, and then press well with the iron from both sides.

16 Gather between the notches on the center top of the smock front body. Refer to the section, "A Small Gathering," in Chapter 4 for tips. Gather the edge until it has decreased enough to match the "finished" gather point when you compare it to pattern piece **10C**. Repeat on the top edge of the body back.

17 Zigzag-stitch the side edges of the body front and body back pieces.

18 With the *right* sides together, sew the smock front body to the smock back body at the side seams with a $5/8$" seam allowance. Press the seams open.

19 With the *right* sides together and starting at the top edge of the body front, sew the bias seam binding strip to the curve of the lower armhole with a $5/8$" seam allowance. Stretch the bias strip ever so slightly as you sew it along the curve. Trim off any excess bias strip beyond the body back top edge.

20 Trim this seam allowance to ¼" and press the bias and the seam allowance up (a). Now wrap the top edge of the bias down to meet the seam line on the *wrong* side, (b). and then fold the entire encased seam down again to the *wrong* side, leaving the seam at the very top edge of the fold. Sew this binding in place about ¼" away from the edge (c).

21 Repeat Steps 19 and 20 on the other side with the remaining bias strip. Press both sides well.

22 Fold and pin the bottom edges of the yoke facings back against their own *right* sides on the front.

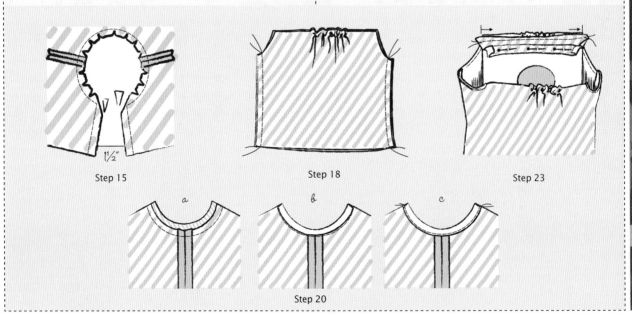

Step 15

Step 18

Step 23

a

b

c

Step 20

23 With the *right* sides together, align the top edges of the smock body front with the bottom edges of the yoke front, centering the body within the yoke and leaving the ⅝" seam allowance on either end of the yoke extending out on either side. Pin in place and sew with a ⅝" seam allowance. Take care not to catch any of the yoke front facing in this seam.

24 Now fold in the ⅝" bottom edge of front yolk facing inward toward the *wrong* side and against the seam allowance that you just made. Press this edge and all seam allowances upward, encasing them within the layers of the yoke and its facing. Pin them together.

25 With the *right* sides together, sew the center edges of the back yoke pieces together with a ⅝" seam allowance until you close the open 1½" bottom edge (a). Repeat with the center back of the back yoke facings (b).

26 Repeat Steps 23 and 24 on the bottom edges of the back yoke sides (a) and the top edge of the smock back body (b). The only difference will be that you need to align the two finished edges of the center back, right up against one another in the seam.

27 You can now whip-stitch or blind-stitch the bottom edge of the facings to the seam allowance by hand. Take care to only sew through the facing and the seam allowance, so that none of your finishing stitches will be visible from the *right* side. See Chapter 5 for instructions on how to do both of these stitches. Press well.

28 Roll-hem the bottom edge of the smock (once you're positive you have the right length less ½" for the hem) by folding in the bottom edge toward the *wrong* side ¼", and then another ¼" to encase the raw edge in the fold, and press. Topstitch ⅛" away from the bottom edge of the smock. Press again.

29 Sew the button on the opposite side of the yoke back from the button loop. Check the section, "Hole-y Buttons," in Chapter 5 for tips.

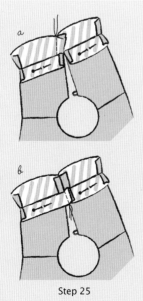

Step 25

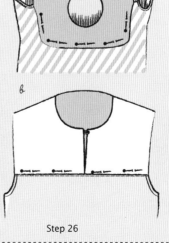

Step 26

Sideways Squares Skirt

Since one size never really fits all, we'll build this skirt from the ground up, based on your very own measurements. You'll do more than make a skirt, you'll also make the pattern! This pattern can be as form-fitting, loosey-goosey, simple, elaborate, long, or short as you'd like it to be, with a simple tweak here and there.

Supplies

FABRIC

- 1½ yards of 44" fabric for knee length
- 3 yards of 54" to 60" fabric for ankle length

Craft scissors

Fabric scissors or rotary cutter and mat

½" elastic

Pencil and marker

Measuring tape

Yardstick

Masking tape (optional)

Calculator (optional, unless you're mathematically inclined)

MY COLOR NOTES

In the skirts shown, I played out a different color-family palette with each skirt. For the square patches, I mixed various charming small-scale prints for a playful and light-hearted look.

There are four basic sections we'll go through to make this skirt: measuring, calculating the pattern size, drawing the pattern, and finally cutting and sewing the skirt. But first read the following paragraph for tips on sewing on the bias.

Bias Tips

As explained in Chapter 3, fabric that is cut on the bias will behave differently than fabric that is cut on the grain or crossgrain. It will "give" or stretch, but not in the same way that a knit fabric will stretch. So, if your skirt is too tight, you could be left with a hemline that is less than even all the way around. It's important when sewing a bias-cut garment to cut the garment large enough to allow the material to "drop" off your figure a bit. Also, when you are running the side seams through the sewing machine, don't tug on the material too much. This will stretch out your side seams and may cause a rippling effect down the sides of the skirt. You'll want to gently guide the material from the front of the needle and not pull from behind the needle as you sew. You may also try tightening the tension on your machine just a bit.

Determine Your Measurements

Be sure to wear form-fitting, thin clothing when taking your measurements, like a camisole and leggings. I find that it's helpful to mark your waistline and hip measurement first by actually taping a strip of masking tape around the circumference of your waist and hips. Make the tape snug against your form, but not so binding that you'll get an inaccurate measurement.

With the waist measurement, be sure to place the tape where you actually want the waist of the skirt to sit. The classic waist measurement is level with the navel, and this is usually where your waist is smallest. You may, however, want your skirt to sit lower than that, so tape/measure at your desired level.

With the hip measurement, you must measure the fullest/widest part of your hip (which is usually where your rear sticks out the most, to put it plainly!).

1 Measure your waistline and write the measurement here:_____inches.

2 Measure your hips and write the measurement here:_____inches.

3 Measure the distance from the waistline to the hipline and write the measurement here:_____inches.

Note: If you've marked yourself with tape first, take the above measurement from the middle of each piece of tape.

4 Measure the length from the waistline to your desired length level (that is, above the knee, below the knee, mid-calf, etc.) and write your measurement here:_____inches.

Calculate and Draw the Pattern

5 Take your waist measurement and divide it by 4, add 1, and then write that result here:_____

(Example: 30-inch waist divided by 4 = 7.5, add 1 =8.5)

6 Take your hip measurement and divide it by 4, add 1, and then write that result here:_____

7 Take your length measurement (Step 4), add 2, and then write that result here:_____

Using the answers from Steps 4, 5, 6, and 7, we'll now draw your skirt pattern. Start with a pencil.

8 Lay your craft paper on a tabletop alongside a yardstick, or along the measurement grid of your cutting mat. The side edge of the paper will be considered the center-fold line of your pattern. So you can write "fold" along the edge.

9 At the side edge of the paper, make a "top" mark, and from that mark, measure a distance equal to the length measurement result from Step 7. Make a "bottom" mark to note that distance.

10 Measuring along the side again, make a "hipline" mark by measuring the distance from the top mark down to a point equal to the waistline-to-hipline distance result in Step 3.

11 At the top mark and using a straightedge, draw a straight, perpendicular line from the side of the paper, ending at a distance equal to your result in Step 5.

12 At the hip-line mark, draw a straight, perpendicular line from the side of the paper, ending at a distance equal to your result in Step 6.

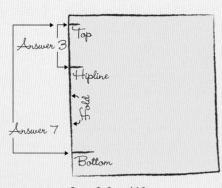

Steps 8, 9, and 10

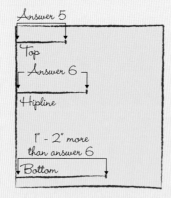

Steps 11, 12, and 13

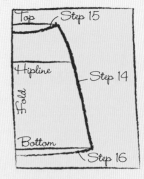

Steps 14, 15, and 16

13 At the bottom-line mark, draw a straight, perpendicular line from the side of the paper, ending at a distance that is an inch or two longer than your result in Step 6. This will determine how full your skirt is at the bottom. If your skirt is anywhere from above the knee to mid-calf or so, you're safe with just going an additional inch or two past the hip width measurement. If you have a longer ankle-length skirt, it will need to be fuller to accommodate walking, at least 3" more than the hip-line width result in Step 6.

14 To finish the pattern, you basically need to connect the dots, but not with point-to-point straight lines. From the outer end of the top line, through the outer end of the hip-line and to the outer end of the bottom line, you should draw one continuous, slightly curved line. This takes a little practice to perfect, but in general, you don't want to make any sudden curves or angles in the side seam line. Think of it as shaping a smooth pattern line to accommodate the measurements within it.

15 With the same smooth line drawing, you'll now draw smooth top and bottom lines from the fold line to the side seam line. At the fold line (paper edge), start your line by dropping down just below the top line about an inch or so, and make a continuous curved line going up to meet the top side-seam point.

16 Draw the bottom line from the fold line (paper edge) to the side-seam line in the same manner as Step 15.

17 Once all your final lines are drawn, trace with a marker over the lines you made in Steps 14, 15, and 16.

18 Using craft scissors, cut out your paper pattern on the marker lines.

Prepare the Pattern Pieces

It should be noted that when drafting your own pattern, it never hurts to have some inexpensive muslin around to try the pattern out with first. Then you won't be wasting your pretty final fabric if you need to make modifications to the fit of the pattern.

19 To ready your fabric to be cut on the bias, lay it out with one selvedge running along the length of your table. Take the opposite top selvedge corner of your fabric and fold it down toward the other selvedge so that the top cut line (make sure it's cut straight on the crossgrain) of the fabric is in line with the selvedge closest to you, forming a triangle-type fold.

20 The line that is noted as the "bias line" in the figure is where you will place the fold line of your skirt pattern. First, smooth out the material to ensure an accurate 45-degree angle of the fold line. Only run your fingers in the direction of the grain or crossgrain of the

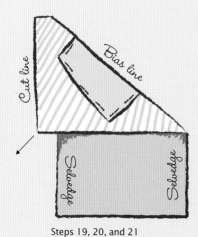

Steps 19, 20, and 21

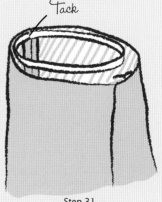

Step 31

fabric when smoothing. Running your fingers along the bias of the fabric may stretch it out of shape.

21 Pin your pattern in place with the pattern's fold line aligned with the fabric's bias line. If your pattern piece is too large to fit within the top triangular space and the fabric lying underneath, continue to pull the top cut line of your material beyond the selvedge closest to you in order to increase the length of the folded bias line. (If the pattern is still too large, you need wider-width fabric.) Be sure to maintain an accurate 45-degree angle.

22 Cut one skirt piece. After the first piece is cut, fold the material as you did in Step 19, but in the opposite direction. Cut a second skirt piece.

23 Finish the side edges of both skirt pieces with a zigzag-stitch (or a serger if you have one) to prevent any raveling.

Make the Square Patches

24 If you don't want to add the squares, skip ahead to Step 27. If you are adding square patches to your skirt, cut them on the grain of the fabric in your desired size plus 1" in each direction.

25 Press ½" of all edges of your squares back to the *wrong* side.

26 Pin the *wrong* side of the squares onto the *right* side of the front piece, the back piece, or both, in your desired arrangement and at an angle so that they look like diamonds. This will keep the grain of the squares consistent with the skirt. Sew them in place on all sides with a straight topstitch, consistently as close to the edge as possible. Any squares that will overlap the side seams cannot be sewn on until after Step 27. Any squares that extend below the bottom edge of the skirt will need to be sewn on after Step 36.

Assemble the Skirt

27 With the *right* sides together, straight-stitch the side seam at a ⅝" seam allowance. Repeat on the opposite side seam. Press both side seams open and try it on to check the fit.

28 After you've made any necessary fit modifications, cut a length of elastic equal to your waist measurement plus 1".

29 Overlap the ends of the elastic by ½" and stitch back and forth several times to secure.

30 On the *wrong* side of the skirt top at one of the side seams, tack the joined elastic down, aligning it with the top edge and with a few stitches.

Stretch →

Tack

Step 32

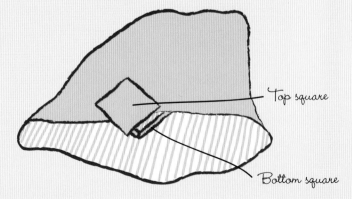

Top square

Bottom square

Step 37

31 Holding the top sides of the skirt with both hands, hook your finger into the elastic loop to stretch it from the tacked-down side to the opposite side seam, and pin it in place at the side seam. Tack elastic to the opposite side seam.

32 Keeping the elastic edge aligned with the skirt top edge, zigzag-stitch the elastic down, all the way around the top, all the while stretching the elastic to accommodate the circumference of the skirt. (I find that using pins makes this step more difficult than not using pins.)

33 Snugly turn down the top edge to the *wrong* side just the width of the elastic, and press.

34 Stitch the turned down edge with a zigzag stitch, stretching a bit as necessary to avoid puckering the material.

35 Press the bottom edge toward the *wrong* side, ½" all the way around. Fold again ½" all around and press a crease.

36 Use the second crease you pressed in Step 35 as your guide to hemming the skirt with a straight stitch ¼" away from the skirt bottom edge. Press.

37 To sew on any squares extending below the bottom edge, cut two squares the same size and press the edges back ½" to their *wrong* sides. Sandwich the skirt edge between the *wrong* sides of the two squares, making sure they mirror each other's placement exactly. Pin together and stitch through all three layers all around the perimeter of the square with a straight stitch.

Bo Peep Skirt

I'd like to think that today's Bo Peep would take a level-headed approach to finding those sheep but still manage to look adorable. Less typical than ruffles-all-the-way-around, this skirt is easy to assemble and gives you a lot of room for mixing around all those cutie-pie prints in your stash.

Supplies

FABRIC

Determined on size, these measurements are for a 4- or 5-year-old:

½ yard, ⅔ yard for front and back

½ yard, ⅔ yard for side panels

⅓ yard for ruffles

¼ yard for trim

½" elastic

Yardstick

Tape measure

Fabric scissors or rotary cutter and mat

MY COLOR NOTES

For Isabela's skirt (left), almost every piece is a different fabric (all from my Garden Party collection) but is unified by shades of blue, citrus yellow, pink, and orange. Hannah's skirt (right) is quieter in color, and I let the print for the main skirt determine a pale pink for the side panels, and a different but still simple floral print for the trim.

Measure and Cut

This skirt is comprised completely from rectangles, based on your child's measurements. There is really no age limit to this skirt. All you need to get started are a waist measurement and the desired finished length for the skirt. Record those measurements below for easy reference.

Waist = _____ inches

Length = _____ inches

1   Cut two rectangles of fabric on the grain for the front and back skirt pieces that are each equal to the waist measurement for the width, and equal to your desired skirt length plus 2" for the length.

2   Cut a third piece for the side panels, the same size as the pieces in Step 1. Now fold the side panel piece in half along the skirt length, and cut along the fold line to end with two equal pieces.

3   For the ruffles, cut four long rectangles that are equal to the entire waist measurement in width by about 5" or 6" or whatever is your desired ruffle length. Keep in mind, about ½" will be rolled into a hem and another ½" will be covered with the ruffle trim.

4   Cut four strips of fabric that are 2" wide and half of the waist measurement in length. These are the ruffle trims.

Assemble the Skirt

5   Make a roll hem on the long bottom edge of all four ruffle pieces by first pressing the edge ¼" toward the *wrong* side, then folding in another ¼" and sewing. Press.

6   Machine-baste the top edge of each of the four ruffle pieces with a ¼" seam allowance, beginning and ending 1" away from the edges.

■

7 Gather the top edge of each of the four ruffles along the basted line until you have reduced their width by half, and it fits across the width of the side panels. Be sure to refer to the section, "A Small Gathering," in Chapter 4 for tips on gathering by hand. (You could also use a ruffling foot on your machine if you have one.)

8 Mark the side panel on each side with your desired ruffle placement, using a yardstick and either pins or tailor's chalk (a). Pin the ruffles' top, gathered edges along those lines, and match up the side edges of the ruffles with the side edges of the side panels (b). You can add as many or as few ruffles as you'd like.

9 Baste each ruffle to the side panels ½" away from the top edge of the ruffle. Also baste the ruffle sides to the side panel sides with a ½" seam allowance. Press the gathers down at the top of the ruffles.

10 Press back both long edges of the ruffle trim strips toward the *wrong* side so that they meet each other. Continue until all four sides are pressed.

11 Layer the *wrong* side of the ruffle trims over the *right* side of the top edge of the ruffles, and pin them in place. Take care to make them level and to cover the seam allowance from the ruffles. Topstitch each ruffle trim on its top and bottom edges. Press well.

12 With the *wrong* sides together, sew the side of one side panel to the side of the skirt front with a ¼" seam allowance. Repeat on the other side of the skirt front with the other side panel. Press the seam allowances to one side.

13 With the *wrong* sides together, sew the side of the skirt back to the side of the side panel. Repeat on the other side of the skirt back with the other side panel, thereby closing the skirt. Press the seam allowances to one side.

14 Now with *right* sides together and keeping the previous seams in the very crease of the fold, sew all the seams again with a $^3/_8$" seam allowance, which will encase the seam allowances from Steps 12 and 13. These are French seams, and you can read a bit more about them in the section, "Seams to You," in Chapter 4. Press the seam allowances well to one side.

15 Now press the bottom edge of the skirt up ¼" toward the *wrong* side. Turn the edge up once more ¼" to make a roll hem all around. Sew about $^1/_8$" from the bottom edge. Press.

16 Turn the top edge toward the *wrong* side about ¼" all around, and press.

17 Now turn this folded edge down again ¾" toward the *wrong* side of the fabric, and pin it in place all around. Topstitch this edge down $^1/_8$" away from the folded bottom edge, and stop just 3" or 4" short of where you began, leaving an opening in the casing.

Side panel

Step 7

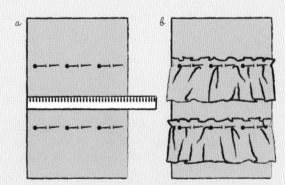

Step 8

Add the Elastic

18 Cut a piece of ½"-wide elastic that is equal to the waist measurement plus 1" or 2".

19 Tack one end of the elastic to the inside fold of the open part of the casing that you made in Step 17 with a few machine stitches. (These stitches will be removed in the next step.) Using either a bodkin or an extra-large safety pin in the other end of the elastic, feed it through the casing until you bring it out on the other side.

20 Making sure that the elastic has not twisted inside the casing, remove the tacking stitches from Step 19, overlap the ends of the elastic by about ½", and machine-sew across both layers of elastic several times.

21 Let the elastic loop slip back into the casing. Evenly spread the gathers created by the elastic back on either side of the open casing area. Pin the casing in place and close it with a final length of topstitching, being careful to avoid sewing over the elastic and joining the previous beginning and ending points of stitching. A final pressing will do it!

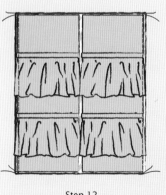

Step 12

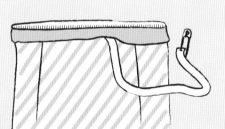

Step 19

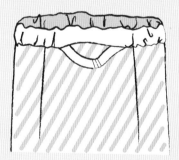

Step 20

Prairie Blouse

What could be sweeter than your little pumpkin frocked in a romantic blouse that looks like it could have been worn by a girl from any century in any country, from Mexico to Holland? The design and construction are so straightforward that you'll want to make one blouse from each of your favorite fabrics. The lofty comfort leaves her plenty of wiggle-room to gallop and giddy-up while she's also busy being irresistibly precious. It's a full-time job on the prairie, ya know.

Supplies

FABRIC
   1½ yard fabric
   3 yards bias strips

¼" elastic
Fabric scissors or rotary cutter
      and mat

MY COLOR NOTES

I really didn't want the shape of this little blouse to be overwhelmed by a print, and so I chose a solid, muted lavender. This cotton has a slight iridescent quality that accents the folds beautifully. Never leaving well enough alone, of course, I had to add a dash of happiness with a kicky trim print, resulting in an unexpected palette when paired with the lavender.

Modify the Pattern's Size

Beyond the size provided, this pattern is easily scaled to a smaller or larger size. To increase the width of the body, place the fold of the fabric a small distance away from the fold line edge of pattern piece **13A** (a). By placing the fold line of pattern piece **13B** a small distance away from the fold of your fabric, you will mostly be increasing the shoulder and neckline opening, and at the same time making the sleeve slightly fuller (b). You may also want to increase the length of the body or the sleeve, by just adding a few inches to the bottom ends of each piece. You could also extend the width of the body and armhole opening by continuing to extend the diagonal line of both the shoulder seam of the sleeve and the shoulder seam of the body (c). These two lines need to be the same length. All these examples of resizing are shown below.

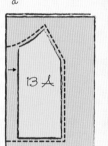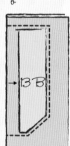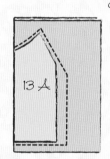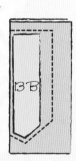

To scale the pattern to a smaller size, you would basically do the opposite. You would fold in the fold line of pattern piece **13A** before placing it against the fold of the fabric for a more narrow body. For a smaller neckline and a narrower sleeve, you would fold in the fold line of pattern piece **13B**. Shortening the diagonal lines of the shoulder seams, by folding in the side of the body and the underside of the sleeve, would decrease the fullness of the sleeve, raise the height of the armhole opening, and decrease the size of the armhole opening. This would also decrease the width of the body a bit. Of course, you can just fold up the ends of the sleeve and the ends of the bottom edge to shorten either of those lengths. You can also wait until after the blouse is sewn together and before you make the sleeve cuffs to trim off any unwanted length in both the sleeves and the body.

Cut

1 Cut pattern piece **13A** from Pattern Page 9, and **13A** (continuation) and **13B** from Pattern Page 10, with craft scissors. Tape the two parts of **13A** together, as instructed on the pattern.

2 Cut two pieces from pattern **13A** on the fold for the front and back (which are interchangeable).

3 Cut two pieces from pattern **13B** on the fold for the sleeves.

4 Cut and join as many 2"-wide bias strips as necessary for about 3 yards of bias, or more if you're enlarging the pattern. Be sure to look at the section, "Maybe I'm Bias," in Chapter 4 for tips on cutting and joining bias strips.

Begin Sewing

5 Zigzag-stitch the edges of the body shoulders and sides, and the sleeve shoulders and undersides as pointed out above. (If you have a serger, you could finish them by overcasting, but not trimming any off.)

6 With the *right* sides together, sew one of the sleeves to the body at the shoulder seam with a ⁵/₈" seam allowance, backstitching at the beginning and end. Repeat at the other shoulder seam with the other sleeve.

7 With the *right* sides together, join the other body piece to one of the sleeves at the shoulder seam with a ⁵/₈" seam allowance, backstitching at the beginning and end. Do not sew the last shoulder seam. Press the three seams open.

8 Turn the long edge of the bias strip back toward the *wrong* side of the fabric ½", and press a crease along the entire length.

9 Starting at the open shoulder seam and with *right* sides together, align the unpressed edge of the bias against the top edge of the neckline, letting a small amount of the bias extend pass the shoulder's edge, and sew the bias to the neckline all the way around with a ½" seam allowance. Stretch the bias, ever so slightly, onto the neckline as you go. Trim off the remaining bias at the end.

10 Press the bias and seam allowances up. With the *right* sides together, close the remaining shoulder seam, including the bias in this seam (unfold the crease from Step 8) with a ⁵/₈" seam allowance. Be sure that the bias seams from Step 9 are lining up with one another in the shoulder seam. Press this seam open.

11 Beginning just past the last shoulder seam that you have sewn, turn the crease edge of the bias in toward the *wrong* side of the blouse and line it up against the bias stitch line, encasing all neckline seam allowances. Begin sewing the folded bias down in

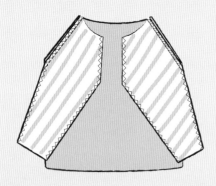

Step 6

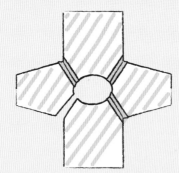

Step 7

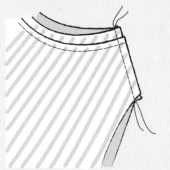

Step 10

place all around the neckline, keeping your stitch line consistently right on the edge of the bias fold and next to the stitch line. Stop sewing a few inches away from where you began. Press.

12 With the *right* sides together, align the unpressed edge of the remaining bias strip with the bottom edge of the sleeve, and sew with ½" seam allowance. Trim excess bias off and use to repeat on the other sleeve. Press all seam allowances at the cuff up toward the bias. Trim the bias in to be in line with the sleeve sides.

13 Starting at the end of one sleeve's bias (which you should unfold the crease of), and with the *right* sides together, align sleeve edges and begin sewing toward the armhole, with a $5/8$" seam allowance, and be sure those cuff allowances stay pressed up toward the bias. When you get to the juncture of the sleeve and the body, stop with your needle down in the shoulder seams, lift the presser foot, turn the fabric to continue down the side of the body, lower the foot, and continue until the bottom of the body and backstitch. Nip the seam allowances near the intersection of the shoulder seams and the side seam. Press the seam open.

14 Open the blouse to the *right* side and lay it out with either side facing up. On the side that has the finished side seam, make a chalk mark or place a pin in the side seam just below the armhole. Measure the distance between this mark and the bottom edge of the body. Now on the other unfinished side, measure that same distance from the bottom up and make another mark on the other side seam below the armhole. Spread the blouse as flat as possible, lay a straightedge across the blouse connecting the two chalk marks, and make a few more marks along the straight line. Flip the blouse over and repeat on the other *right* side of the blouse. This can also be done with pins, instead of chalk.

15 With the remaining bias strip, fold in the unfolded edge toward the *wrong* side until it almost reaches the first crease of the other edge, and press. (At this point, also be sure that your bias strip is long enough to fit around the front and the back of the blouse. Add to it to increase the length, if necessary.)

16 Starting at the open side seam, lay the *wrong* side of the folded and pressed bias strip against the *right* side of the blouse body, aligning of the top edge of the bias strip with the chalk lines. Pin it in place all the way around to the other side of the open side seam.

17 Topstitch the very top edge of the bias to the blouse all the way around. Repeat on the very bottom edge of the bias.

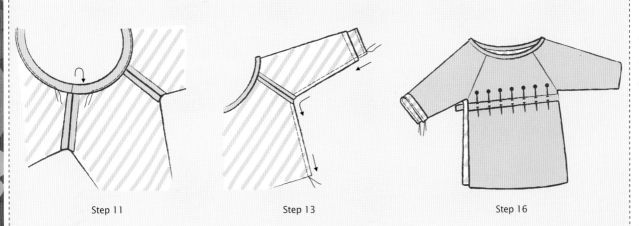

Step 11   Step 13   Step 16

18 Starting at the cuff of the remaining sleeve, and with the *right* sides together, sew the sleeve seam with a ⅝" seam allowance toward the lower shoulder seam. Stop with the needle down in the shoulder seam, turn the fabric to sew down along the side, and sew just a bit more—stopping where the top bias stitching is and starting again at the lower bias stitching to finish at the bottom of the blouse. Be sure that you leave the small distance between the bias stitching lines in this side seam open. Nip the seam allowances near the intersection of the shoulder seams and the side seams. Press them open.

Add the Elastic and Finishing

19 With either a bodkin or a safety pin pinned through the ¼" elastic, feed a length of elastic through the neckline bias opening to gather up the neckline to your desired size. Sew the ends together with several stitches back and forth, trim off the excess elastic, and let it slip into place.

Note: You may want to have your little pumpkin-doodle nearby to hold it up against her, checking how gathered you'd like the neck to be while the ends of the elastic are just pinned together. Having one of her existing blouses nearby is also helpful.

20 Push the gathers to each side of the opening out of the way, in order to close the opening of the bias casing, connecting your previous sewing beginning and ending points.

21 On each sleeve cuff, turn the folded edge of the bias toward the *wrong* side, and line it up next to the stitch line that attached the bias, thereby encasing the seam allowances. Sew down all around just inside the edge of the bias, stopping an inch or so from where you started.

22 Feed elastic through and finish these bias casings on the sleeves, in the same manner that you did in Steps 19 and 20 for the neckline.

23 From the *wrong* side of the blouse, feed elastic through the bias casing on the blouse body, making it as gathered as you wish. Pull both ends out and safety-pin them together a bit to the outside of the side seam. Return the side seam to the sewing machine, and close the side seam opening with a few stitches and backstitches that will also sew the elastic ends in place. Trim off the elastic.

24 Roll-hem the bottom of the blouse by turning the edge toward the *wrong* side ¼" twice, and stitching ⅛" away from the edge. Press the blouse well.

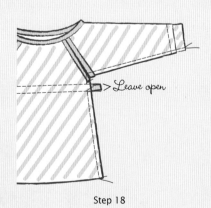

Step 18

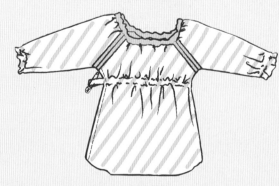

Step 23

Chapter 8
Decorate

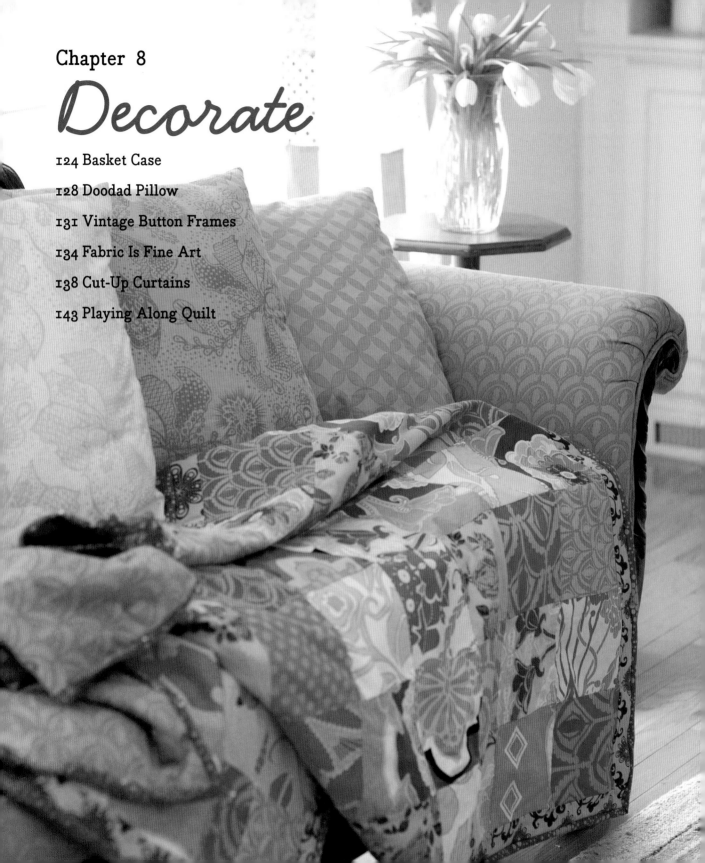

Basket Case

Gather up a few of your favorite fabrics for this little lovely. This pillowcase made for a long-back pillow employs simple gathering techniques that alternate their direction to emulate a basket weave. The effect is just as pretty using two fabrics as it is using one single, solid-colored fabric.

Supplies

FABRIC

- 15 rectangles measuring 6" x 10" (If you want to alternate two fabrics, you'll need eight of one fabric and seven of the other fabric.)
- ½ yard fabric for back
- 1 yard of white cotton muslin for inner pillow

Fiberfill

Fabric scissors or rotary cutter and mat

Yardstick

Hand-sewing needle

MY COLOR NOTES

I chose a duo of small, vintage-inspired prints for this pillow. They are different both in color and in how crowded the print is, but the dominant coral background of one fabric relates to some of the blossoms on the other.

Cut

1   Cut 15 rectangles of fabric for the front pieces, measuring 6" x 10" (if alternating two fabrics, cut eight from one fabric and cut seven from the other fabric).

2   Cut two pieces of fabric for the pillowcase back, measuring 16" x 18".

3   Cut two pieces of cotton muslin, measuring 16" x 26".

Assemble the Inner Pillow Form

4   Starting roughly at the center of the longer sides, sew the two pieces of cotton muslin together, all around the perimeter with a ½" seam allowance. Stop sewing about 4" or 5" from where you started, leaving an opening.

5   Clip off the corners of the seam allowance, turn the *right* side out, and press.

6   Stuff the form with fiberfill until it's evenly plump.

7   Close the opening using a simple, hand-sewn whip stitch since it is an inner pillow that won't be seen; but you can certainly use a blind stitch if you really want to. Both styles of hand-stitching are shown in Chapter 5. Set it aside.

Gather the Front Pieces

8   Set the stitch length on your sewing machine to a long basting stitch. Starting ½" from the end of the 10" side of the rectangle and using a ¼" seam allowance, baste along one edge, stopping ½" away from the edge. Don't cut the threads, but pull the piece back so that you have a thread slack of about 8" or 9".

Note: The chain piecing method that is used in Steps 9 and 10 is a real time saver, but you could baste the two 10" sides of all of the rectangles individually if you prefer.

9 Repeat this basting stitch on the next rectangle and the rest to create a chain, always going down the long side of the rectangle and putting about 8" or 9" of thread slack between the pieces. Cut the end threads when you finish the last rectangle.

10 Turn the chain and repeat down the other 10" sides of the rectangles.

11 Once you have basted all of the 10" sides, clip the threads at about halfway between the pieces, so that you are left with 15 individual pieces.

12 With one of the rectangles, at one end of the basting stitching, tie together the bobbin thread and the top thread in a knot. Repeat on the other side, knotting one end and leaving the opposite end free.

13 Once the threads are knotted on one end, take either the free top thread or the bobbin thread, and begin tugging on it gently like a drawstring to begin gathering up the fabric. (You can refer to the section, "A Small Gathering," in Chapter 4 for practice.) Gather up the edge until you have reduced the length of that 10" side to 6", and then knot the top thread and the bobbin thread together. Repeat on the other side of the rectangle.

14 Repeat this gathering on the rest of the pieces. You may want to press them just lightly to prepare them for assembly.

Assemble the Front and Back Pieces

15 Using the diagram below as a piecing guide, notice that the pieces are arranged so that the direction of the gathers, either horizontal or vertical, alternates as you assemble the pillow front. So one piece will have gathers at the left and right, and then the piece next to it will have gathers at the top and bottom. If you are also alternating between two different fabrics, the fabric of which you have eight pieces should occupy the corner positions of the pillowcase ("A" pieces). The other fabric pieces or "B" pieces will fill in the alternate spots. Try to lay out your pieces on a table first in the correct form. This will help you as you take pieces to the machine to sew together.

16 Making five columns of three pieces, begin pinning pieces *right* sides together, and sewing with a ½" seam allowance. You may notice that the gathered edges have stretched out a little. Gently nudge in those gathers as you sew to be sure that your ends are matching up. Continue in sets of three until you have made five columns.

17 Now with the *right* sides together and sewing with a ½" seam allowance, assemble one column to the next, in the correct order, making sure that your seams match at the square intersections. Continue until all of the columns are joined and thereby completing your pillow front.

Step 4

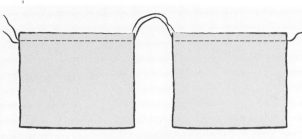

Step 9

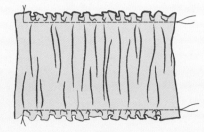

Step 13

18 With a pillow back piece, press back a ½" allowance toward the *wrong* side of the fabric on just one of the 16" edges.

19 Fold back that pressed edge ½" once more, and sew a hem. Repeat on the other pillow back piece.

20 Lay the pillow front *right* side up. Lay down one pillow back piece *right* side down on top of the pillow front, with the hemmed edge at the center and the other edge lining up with the edge of the pillow front. Repeat with the other back piece on the opposite end, layering on top. Pin all around. You may again have to ease in some of the gathers for the pillow front to fit it well onto the pillow back.

21 Sew around the entire perimeter of the pillowcase with a ½" seam allowance. Clip the corners, turn the *right* side out, and press.

22 Insert the inner pillow form you've made through the overlapping back piece of the pillowcase.

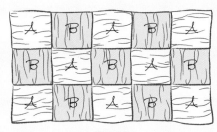

Step 15

Step 16

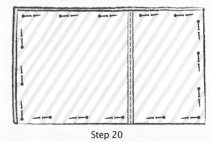

Step 20

Doodad Pillow

The Doodad Pillow is a chance to do something crafty and creative with all the trims that are too short for a skirt, one-and-only funky buttons, and weird lime-green lace you *mistakenly* thought was pretty. This pillow lines up all these misfits into an orderly monogram pillow. So if you have a knickknack box that's overflowing, this pillow is calling your name. Well, it's at least calling the first letter of your name.

Supplies

FABRIC

$2/3$ yard of fabric at least 44" in width

18" x 18" pillow form

Assorted trims, buttons, yo-yos, rosettes, etc. of your choice

Lightweight and sheer fusible interfacing, measuring roughly 20" x 20"

Fabric scissors or rotary cutter and mat

Yardstick

Hand-sewing needle

Air-soluble marker or tailor's chalk

MY COLOR NOTES

This pillow joins together some of my favorite vintage buttons and a flower that my daughter crocheted one day when we were teaching ourselves some new tricks. The background colors were not too hard to work with since they are so unique to begin with, so I just instinctively made choices after layering on a few things to "audition" the pieces for my pillow.

1   Cut two squares of fabric measuring 20½" x 20½", from either the same or different fabrics.

2   Print out from your computer or draw the letter of your choice in the size of your choice. Be sure to consider your pillow size when determining the size of your letter.

3   Tape the letter facing you to a window during sunlight hours. Center your pillow front fabric over the letter with the *right* side facing you, and tape it in place so that it's pretty taut. A light box also works great, if you have one.

4   Mark the fabric in several places to trace the shape of the letter with either an air-soluble marker or tailor's chalk.

Note: If your fabric is too thick or dark to see the letter through, cut the letter out and center it on the *right* side of the pillow front; pin all along the inside of the letter, following the shape. Then gently tear the paper off, making sure the pins stay in place.

5   Fuse the lightweight interfacing onto the wrong side of the pillow front, following the manufacturer's directions.

6   Begin arranging your "doodads" and elements on top of the pins to "draw" the letter out with your various materials. Fit different elements together snugly and without large gaps, so that the letter is legible.

7   Once you've achieved your desired placement, move the layout onto the printed-out letter in the same order so that you won't forget it. Keep it nearby, and then, piece by piece, begin hand-sewing on your elements.

Note: Refer back to Chapters 4 and 5 for different techniques on hand-sewing trims, buttons, and bias strips, or for making gathers and various embroidery stitches. Also learn to make a yo-yo in the "Opposites Attract" project in Chapter 6. Just eliminate inserting the cardboard into the yo-yo from the magnet project to adapt it for this project. Also if you are more comfortable using an embroidery hoop for the hand-sewing, have at it.

8 After all the elements have been sewn in place, it's time to begin the pillow assembly. With the *right* sides together, sew the front and back pieces together with a ½" seam allowance on three sides continuously. When you come to a corner: stop ½" away from the edge, leave the needle down, lift the foot, turn the fabric, lower the foot, and continue along the next edge. Backstitch at the beginning and end.

9 Clip the two corners of the pillow that are sewn.

10 Fold down ½" of the open edge of the pillowcase all the way around, *wrong* sides together, and press a crease with the iron.

11 Turn the pillowcase *right* side out, and insert the pillow form. Slide the case around and fluff the form until it fits smoothly.

12 Align the creased edges of the opening together, and pin them shut.

13 Close the pillow's opening using a blind stitch, as explained in Chapter 5.

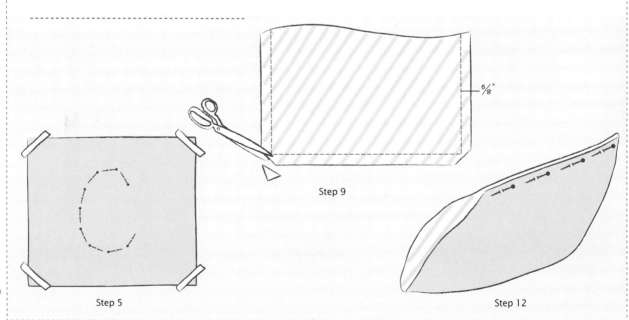

Step 5

Step 9

Step 12

5/8"

Vintage Button Frames

If you've been collecting old buttons that you are afraid to put on a garment for fear of breaking or losing them, this is your project. The buttons do not have to be old, of course, but something you feel like showing off. Also, this project will give a home to some small cuts of your favorite fabrics, and those unused frames that you've had lying around. Beware that these little ditties look quite cozy in groupings—go ahead and plan out several.

Supplies

FABRIC

- Fabric that is at least 2" bigger in width and length than the frame's opening
- Heavy interfacing at least as large as the frame's opening (fusible or non-fusible)

- Picture frame of any size or material (but a small, wooden frame is recommended)
- Frame backing or cardboard, if not already with the frame
- Many (or just a few) buttons of any size or color
- Ruler
- Fabric scissors or rotary cutter and mat
- Hand-sewing needle
- Air-soluble fabric marker

MY COLOR NOTES

My color decisions were based on how the buttons should interplay with the fabric. In most of these, I wanted the buttons to either stand out boldly against the fabric, or to work into the design of the fabric and just add sparkle. They were each like little works of art with their own compositions and ideas behind them, and so I went about the color process very instinctively.

1 Remove all backings, glass, and table stands from the frame. Determine the frame space dimension by measuring the frame opening from the back.

Note: Don't measure the window that you see from the front; measure from the back so that the lip around the window is included.

2 Cut a piece of heavy interfacing that is $1/8$" smaller in both directions than the frame space. If you have a frame with a unique shape like an oval, circle, or hexagon, you'll have to trace out the frame opening and double-check the fit by placing it into the frame back. It should fit well, with a little wiggle room for the fabric.

3 Lay the cut interfacing down on your fabric and cut the fabric out around the shape, leaving an extra border of about 1" all the way around.

4 Place the fabric *right* side down on the ironing board with the interfacing centered on top of it. Start wrapping each side of the fabric back against the interfacing snugly, and press all the edges to make a crease.

5 Pin the overlapping corners of the fabric to hold them smoothly in place. Check the fit of the fabric wrapped piece in the frame. It should be snug, but not so tight that it buckles from squeezing it in. Also, it shouldn't be too small, causing it to slide back and forth.

6 Topstitch the perimeter of the fabric and interfacing as close as possible to the edge, removing the pins as you go. Backstitch over your beginning stitches.

7 Give it an extra pressing from the front side to smooth out the fabric and stitches.

8 Arrange the buttons of your choice in any configuration you like on top of the fabric form. Move them around randomly, or place them in a design or perhaps in the form of a monogram.

9 Once you've decided on an arrangement, carefully put a dot underneath each button with an air-soluble fabric marker. If you're creating an arrangement like a monogram, you might want to mark that out by hand with some long basting stitches. If your arrangement is intricate or if you don't have a fabric pen, you can re-create the arrangement on top of double-stick tape that's stuck to a piece of cardboard of the same size so that you don't forget the placement.

10 Begin sewing on the buttons one-by-one using the tips from "Hole-y Buttons" in Chapter 5. (For this application, you will not need to create a shank with thread, as described in Chapter 5, because the buttons will be only decorative.)

11 If you marked with long basting stitches in Step 9, remove them gently.

12 Place your new vintage button art into the frame and replace the frame's backing. If your frame was originally a tabletop frame with a stand and you want it to hang on the wall, replace the previous backing or stand with a simple taped-in piece of cardboard. Add a picture hanger.

Step 1

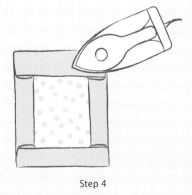

Step 4

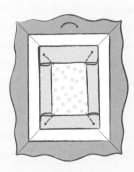

Step 5

Fabric Is Fine Art

Poke those needles back into the pin cushion. Wind that dangling thread nice and tidy around the spool. Turn off the sewing machine. It's art time. Open up a book of Georgia O'Keefe paintings or Henri Matisse paper cutouts. Flip through a garden magazine for some floral inspiration. Or take your camera around the house, and set up some vignettes of fruit in a bowl or flowers in a vase. Better yet, draw. Draw something simple and wonderful . . . a butterfly, a bird, or an apple. This project uses fabric and your imagination to create art for your wall. So take your time coming up with the right image, and the pieces of this process will fall together perfectly.

Supplies

FABRIC

Various scraps of fabric

Cotton muslin, somewhat sheer, measuring 10" larger in both directions than the artist canvas

Light-weight, double-sided fusible web (Steam-A-Seam sheets are excellent)

Pre-stretched artist canvas in the size of your choice

An inspirational drawing, photograph, or artwork

Tracing paper

Craft or masking tape

Fabric scissors

Craft scissors

Permanent marker

Pencil or air-soluble fabric marker

Computer printer or color copies

Staple gun and staples

Yardstick

Clear acrylic gel medium (optional; can use Mod-Podge)

Craft paintbrush (optional)

MY COLOR NOTES

The colors and fabric that I chose for this project were completely based on the image that I decided to base my "art" on. For instance, the red of the tomatoes inspired me to choose a small red print. I really enjoyed using a mix of little prints and some solids for this piece to awaken the composition into something warm and meaningful, almost like a quilt. Instead of fabric swatch, here is the inspiration photo for this project.

Tips on Finding the Inspirational Image

Find an image or composition that you would like to replicate with pieced fabric. What you will essentially be making is a puzzle of various fabrics resembling an image. When drawing, photographing, or borrowing a suitable image, look for something with rather large shapes and components. Each of these shapes will be broken down and replicated with a piece of fabric and then recomposed like a puzzle. We'll be cutting and fusing the shapes next to each other, and so fussy little pieces will be harder to deal with. You might consider deciding on your image first before you buy the canvas. If you decide to use a square image, you'll want to find a square canvas, etc. You will be enlarging the image to fit your canvas size either by printing from the computer or at a copy store, and so getting the dimensions right will also be important.

Preparing the Art Layout

1 Laying tracing paper over your inspirational image, trace the general shapes with a pencil. Take some time doing this, and eliminate details that are not essential to the overall flow of the image. Below is an example of how my photograph gets transformed into line art with this process. Draw around the shapes of forms, but also around the areas of color, for instance, the highlight on the tomato. Once you have the lines the way you want them, trace over the pencil with a black permanent marker.

2 Make an enlargement of the line drawing to the dimension that matches your canvas. If you have a printer, you may need to "tile" the image together with several sheets of copy paper. Accurately tape the tiles together with clear tape, front and back, before moving on.

Note: If you need to go to a copy store to enlarge your image, let a clerk help you—that's why they're there. Just be sure you can tell them what your final size should be. You also can make copies to tape together, as mentioned in Step 2, if you don't want to pay for an oversized print.

3 Lay the canvas centered on top of the drawing on tracing paper, making sure that all of your drawing fits underneath the perimeter of the canvas. Trace the outline of the canvas onto your drawing with a permanent marker. You should now have a line border around your drawing.

4 Using your inspirational piece as a guide, write into each shape the general color you'd like to use for it. This will be like your color map when choosing the fabrics for each shape. You may want to add descriptive words with the colors, like "dark red" or "dull blue," to give yourself extra hints when choosing fabrics. The writing will also keep you from flipping the piece of paper backward when cutting out the fabric because you'll have it as a guide to check for the *right* side.

Prepare the Background

5 Cut out the muslin larger than the drawing and canvas size, so that there is a 5" border of extra fabric all around.

6 Center the canvas on the muslin, and lightly trace the perimeter of the canvas onto the muslin with a pencil or an air-soluble fabric marker.

7 Tape your drawing down to the tabletop, just at the corners. Lay the muslin over the drawing, lining up the perimeter drawn on the muslin with the perimeter of the drawing, and tape the corners down to hold in place. Trace the lines of the drawing with a pencil or an air-soluble fabric marker. This only needs to be a light tracing. Be careful not to stretch the fabric as you trace.

Step 1

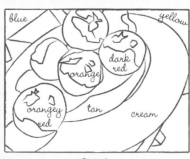

Step 4

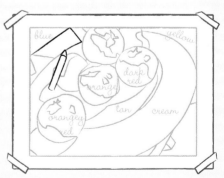

Step 7

8 Lay the muslin drawing side up over a piece of double-sided fusible web cut to the size of your picture dimension, and press with an iron to fuse. (Be sure to follow the manufacturer's directions for the particular fusible web you have.) Leave on one of the paper backings for now.

Compose Your Fine Art

9 Cut out the pieces of the art "puzzle" you've created on the copy paper. Lay them out, fitted back together, on your worktable.

10 Once you've determined the fabrics you'll be using for each piece, go ahead and adhere some of the fusible web to the back of those fabrics. Only remove one of the backings to do this and leave the other on. Keep in mind the amount you'll be using of a given fabric, and don't fuse too much more than you need.

Note: There will inevitably be some scraps of fabric with fusible web on the back left over, but you can save them in a baggie for future smaller projects. Fusing the back of the fabric first before cutting out the shapes helps to stabilize the fabric and gives it a cleaner cut edge.

11 Begin using the cut paper pieces from Step 9 as patterns to cut out various shapes from assorted fused fabrics that correspond to the colors that you've noted on each piece. Be sure you are laying the back side of the paper against the *right* side of the fabric before you cut. You'll know you're doing it right if you can still read your color notes on top of each piece. Save your paper pieces, and set them aside.

12 As you cut the fused fabric pieces to your art puzzle, lay them in place on the muslin-covered canvas in their corresponding position. Once you have all the pieces cut and laid out, check for fit and make any fabric changes you wish for your desired outcome.

13 Once you've decided on the final layout, begin peeling the backing off the back side of the fused fabrics and press the pieces onto the muslin-covered canvas.

14 Now fuse the muslin to the canvas, aligning the outer edges carefully. Let the extra fabric border just fall away on the sides for now. You may press from the back of the canvas as well to get a good adhesion.

15 Wrap two opposing sides of muslin around to the back side tightly, and staple the pieces into place with your staple gun. It's best to do this with the canvas lying on a clean table on its front side.

16 Using a bed-corner fold, fold back the remaining opposing sides and staple them in place.

17 Trim any extra muslin that extends within the back opening past the stretcher bars.

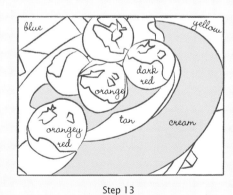
Step 13

Step 15

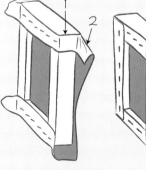
Step 16

Cut-Up Curtains

In this clever curtain project, we will actually be tearing up more than we will be cutting up. But the finished product will evoke a totally hip cut-and-pieced look. The key to this project turning out well is getting a good measurement on your window (or shower stall) and perfecting the art of ripping.

Supplies

FABRIC

Enough yards of solid-colored fabric to cover your window measurement's width and your desired length

Assorted printed fabrics (5 or 6), either scraps or several ½-yard cuts

Self-retracting tape measure (sold at hardware stores)

Tape measure (the sewing kind)

Curtain rod

Fabric scissors or rotary cutter and mat

Yardstick

Masking tape

Fabric chalk or soluble fabric marker

MY COLOR NOTES

I chose the main fabric for this curtain in a pale cream shade so that light could filter through nicely. For the assorted printed fabrics, I chose several vintage-style prints in variations of red, white, brown, and blue. The prints are all light to medium in color and therefore don't overwhelm the composition with boldness, but keep the finished product sweet and soft.

Measure Your Window

This curtain is a rod-pocket style curtain that hangs flat without gathers when it's closed. If you want your curtain to have more fullness or gathers even when pulled shut, then you will need to add to the width measurement. This will often mean either buying wider fabric for the panel or putting a vertical seam in the panel to make it wider. This pattern is not really designed for windows much wider than 48" or so. But if you have an extra-wide window, you could make one for each side of it.

To determine the dimension of the curtain, you will need three different measurements:

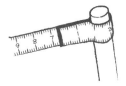

A The measurement of the rod it will hang from. To do this, wrap your sewing tape measure around the rod so that the end of it is pressed against itself on the other side for about an inch. See the figure above.

B The measurement you want the total length of the curtain to be.

C The measurement you want the width of the curtain to be.

Do the Math

Now add measurements A, and B, together and add 1". This number is your length measurement. Next, take measurement C and add 1", and that will be your width measurement. As always, don't forget to wash your fabrics before cutting.

Make the Curtain

1   Using the formula on the previous page, determine the dimensions of your panel piece and cut it out of the solid fabric, being careful to cut it straight on the grain. If you have to piece the fabric across the width to make it wide enough, do this with three pieces of fabric, the center being the widest, and the other two pieces on each side being smaller widths. This way, there is no seam going up the middle of your curtain. Or perhaps you could find a wider width fabric that you like for the background of the panel.

2   Press the side edges in ¼" toward the *wrong* side, all along the length of the panel on both sides.

3   Topstitch the side edges down, turning it back once more ¼" as you sew. Pin it in place first, if that's helpful. Press both sides.

4   Press the top edge down toward the *wrong* side of the panel at ¼".

5   In the same manner that you wrapped the tape measure around the rod (see measurement A on page 139), wrap the *wrong* side of the curtain top around the rod and pin it in place near one of the side edges. Also mark the panel with a pin at the same edge, right under where the bottom of the folded top edge hits the curtain side edge.

6   Remove the rod from the curtain, and remove the pins that are keeping the pocket folded down. Only leave in the pin that is marking where the bottom edge of the rod pocket should stop. Fold the curtain in half lengthwise, and pin a mark on the opposite side to indicate where the rod pocket stops at a matching level to the first pin mark.

7   Open the curtain and lay it flat on a table with the back side facing up. Using a yardstick, draw a chalk line or fabric pen line from one pin to the other.

8   Fold down the top edge to meet this line and pin it in place. Topstitch the fold down very close to the folded edge. Press.

9   Press ¼" of the bottom edge of the curtain to the *wrong* side.

10   To hem the bottom, ideally you would already have the curtain rod hanging so that you can hang the curtain and pin the hem up for accuracy, especially if you want the curtain to hit the floor or any level exactly. If, however, you are not too picky about it, go ahead and topstitch the folded edge up, folding it up one more time as you sew, just as you did in Step 3 for the side edges. Press.

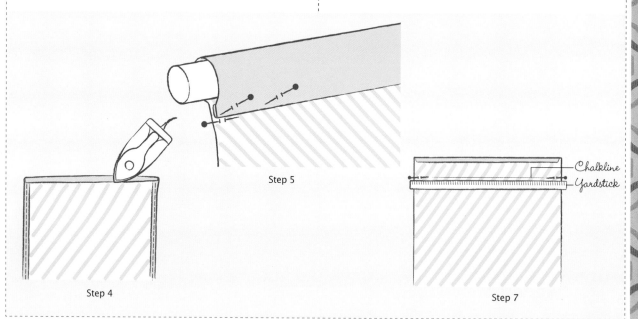

Step 5

Step 4

Step 7

Chalkline
Yardstick

Start Stripping

A quality cotton fabric should rip or tear very easily on the grain or crossgrain of the fabric, giving you a very nice, straight, albeit frayed, edge. The raw edge is desirable for the style of this particular project. There is some slight pulling and stretching that can happen when ripping, but this curtain doesn't take itself too seriously.

11 To make your fabric strips, first wash, dry, and press the printed fabrics of your choice.

12 Because the fabric may not have been cut straight at the store, you'll want to rip off a little bit first, so that you are starting with a straight crosswise edge. All the strips that we will rip will start at one selvedge and rip across to the other selvedge on the crossgrain of the fabric. To do this, lay out your fabric with the selvedge lined up along the side of the table that is closest to you. Go up about 1" or 2" from the cut edge and snip the scissors just through the selvedge.

13 With both hands and applying equal pressure on each side, rip the fabric apart all the way across. You may have to snip with the scissors again once you get all the way across to the opposite selvedge. You don't need to lift the fabric up off the table much to rip it. But once you've grabbed and ripped it, grab closer to the end of the tear and continue. Throw that piece in your scrap pile.

14 Now clip your selvedge every 2½" to rip several strips in equal widths. Continue this on all the fabrics, until you have several strips. Press all the strips to prepare them for sewing. Cut the strips into various lengths.

15 Mark your yardstick with masking tape at the 4", 8", and 12" marks.

16 Lay the yardstick across the panel, aligning the end of it with the curtain edge. Pin the fabric or mark with chalk at 4", 8", and 12" from the edge marks. Slide down the curtain edge a little and repeat so that you are marking what look like three concentric lanes on a racetrack.

17 When you come within 4" of the rod pocket stitching at the top, turn the yardstick in the other direction and use that stitch line as your guide to marking the "tracks" from the top. At the bottom of the panel, you will measure off the three marks from the bottom edge. It's helpful to mark the corners with two pins stuck perpendicular to each other.

18 You can now begin layering strips of material in place for attaching the fabric tracks. Start on the outside track and pin the strips in place to the inside of the 4" marking, all the way around, layering the end of one over the beginning of another.

19 Begin topstitching the strips down ¼" away from the edge, on both edges, all the way around (this means you'll need to sew around each fabric track twice).

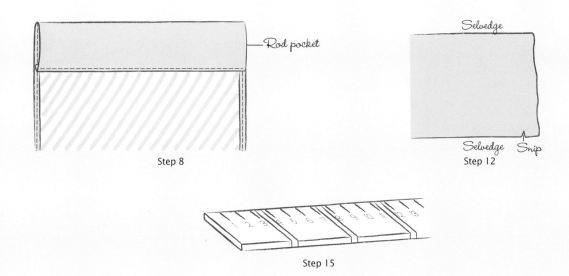

Step 8 — Rod pocket

Step 12 — Selvedge / Selvedge / Snip

Step 15

20 Now go back and stitch down the overlapping ends, ¼" away from the edge of the end on top.

21 Repeat Steps 18, 19, and 20 with the remaining fabric tracks, and press all when finished.

Note: The width of the strips, the number of fabric tracks you sew on, and the space that is in between each strip are completely variable. You may want more strips that are wider if your curtain is really wide, or fewer narrow strips if you curtain is narrow.

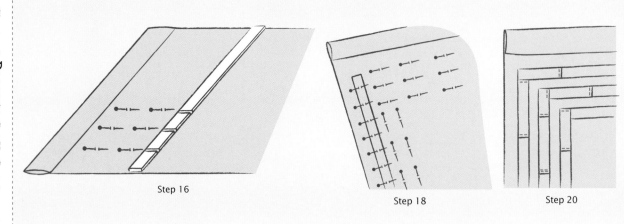

Step 16

Step 18

Step 20

Playing Along Quilt

If you've been intimidated by the notion of quilting, this one is for you. All the circles and squares in this design evoke a playful nostalgia of checkers, bull's-eyes, blocks, and other favorite ways of passing time. This quilt is made up of three different styles of 12" x 12" quilt blocks that are pretty basic. You can then combine any variation of those blocks for a total of 42 blocks in the quilt. Or you could choose to do only one style of block in various fabrics for the whole quilt. Or you can take what you've learned here and simply join squares! Just play along.

Supplies

FABRIC

- 6–7 yards for the pieced front, made up of different cuts of fabric
- 6 yards for the backing
- 2–3 yards for the front border
- 10–11 yards of bias strips (homemade or purchased)

90" x 102" of quilt batting (cotton or cotton blend is recommended)

Rotary cutter and mat with measurements

Straightedge (or quilter's ruler)

Compass

Aluminum foil

Thin poster board

Appliqué needle

Quilt safety pins or regular safety pins

MY COLOR NOTES

Because I wanted this quilt to have an all-American feel to it, I chose a palette that is a twist on red, white, and blue. There are several solid versions of those three colors, in addition to a few interjections of army green and various shades of brown. I used prints sparingly compared to solids for a more modern and graphic effect.

Block Style One

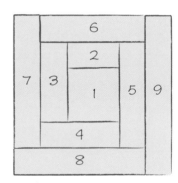

The diagram above shows the layout of the nine different shapes that make up Block Style One. It's a version of what's known as a log cabin block. Each piece is numbered in the order that it should be sewn together.

You may choose to make pattern pieces out of paper or poster board, so that you won't have to measure every time you want to make this block. If you are clever on the computer, you could also create the shapes in a graphics program and print them out. Just double-check the dimensions after it's printed.

1   Cut all the pieces for Block Style One using the following list of dimensions that correspond to the piece numbers, as shown in the diagram above:

1. 4½" x 4½"   4. 2½" x 6½"   7. 2½" x 10½"
2. 2½" x 4½"   5. 2½" x 8½"   8. 2½" x 10½"
3. 2½" x 6½"   6. 2½" x 8½"   9. 2½" x 12½"

2 Sew pieces 1 and 2 together, with the *right* sides together at a ¼" seam allowance. Stitch all the way to the end, and backstitch at the beginning and the end. Press the seam allowance outward toward piece 2.

Note: It's very important to maintain your seam allowance as consistently as possible so that all your quilt blocks will line up correctly. But don't sweat it— it will be beautiful even if it is less than perfect.

3 Sew piece 3 to the left of pieces 1 and 2, with the *right* sides together at a ¼" seam allowance as above, and press outward again.

4 Continue this same process of stitching and pressing according to the order directed by the piece numbers. Be sure that the seam allowances are lying down in the direction you've pressed them when you make each new seam. As long as you are holding the seam allowances down in the outward direction as you add new pieces, you can save the pressing until you've finished the block. Make as many or as few of these blocks as you like, playing around with different color combinations. Set the blocks aside.

Block Style Two

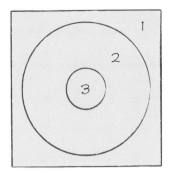

This block layers three shapes together and is quite simple. Refer back to the "Super Circles" in Chapter 5 for tips on making the nice and smooth circles. You should be able to make the circular paper pattern by using a compass. Or, as with the first block, feel free to draft the circles in your graphics program and print it from the computer. The size of these circles will not affect how the quilt comes together at all, so feel free to determine your own size.

5 Cut a 12½" x 12½" fabric square.

6 Cut a fabric circle 10" in diameter.

7 Cut a fabric circle 4" in diameter.

8 Cut a poster board circle 9" in diameter.

9 Cut a poster board circle 3" in diameter

10 Perform the "Super Circles" technique on page 57 on both of the circles, using the poster board circles, foil, and iron to get a nice, smooth edge on the circles.

Step 2

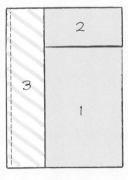

Step 3

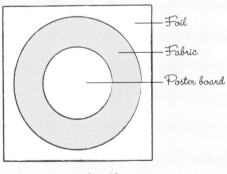

Step 10

11 Center the *wrong* side of the larger circle onto the *right* side of the square and pin it in place. Attach the circle to the square with a blind stitch or a slip stitch (see page 56).

12 Repeat Step 11 with the small circle onto the center of the previous circle. Press. As with Block Style One, make as many or as few of these as you wish. Vary the size of the circles for added interest, or move the center circle off-center for a dance-y look. Set the blocks aside.

You could machine topstitch the circles on, instead of blind-stitching by hand. If you do, keep the stitches extremely and uniformly close to the edge of the circle.

Block Style Three

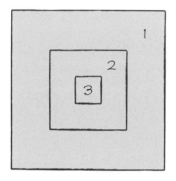

This block appliqués two squares on top of one large one.

13 Cut a 12" x 12" fabric square.

14 Cut a 7" x 7" fabric square.

15 Cut a 3" x 3" fabric square.

16 Press a ¼" fold down toward the *wrong* side of the 7" square all the way around.

17 Pin in the 7" pressed square, *wrong* side in place on the center of the *right* side of the 12" square.

18 Blind stitch it in place by hand.

19 Repeat Steps 16, 17, and 18 with the 3" square. Press. Make as many of these blocks as you wish.

Note: You could machine topstitch the squares on instead of blind-stitching by hand. If you do, keep the stitches extremely and uniformly close to the edge of the circle.

Assembly Meeting

20 Once you have completed all 42 blocks (more or less), it's time to lay them out and start playing. It could be that this process has taken you months and not days, but the best is saved for last. Arrange the blocks in rows of six by seven. Keep an eye on balancing the color throughout the composition of the finished layout.

21 Begin sewing the blocks *right* sides together, the side of one to the side of the next, with a ¼" seam allowance, and continue in horizontal rows of seven. Press the seams open.

22 Once you've joined all the horizontal rows, you can begin assembling the rows with *right* sides together and matching up the block seams as closely as possible. Press the seams open. Continue to Step 23 if you'd like to add a border. Skip to Step 25 if not.

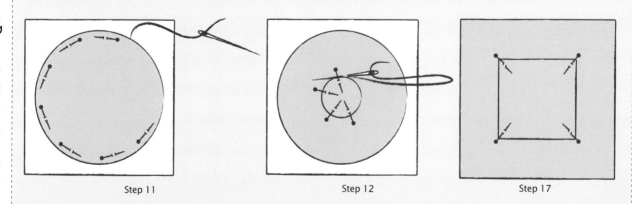

Step 11   Step 12   Step 17

23 Optional: An additional step for the front of the quilt would be to add a border, or a sashing. Cut two strips of fabric that are 3" wide and as long as your quilt. Sew each strip onto the right and left sides of the quilt, with the *right* sides together at a ¼" seam allowance. Press the seams open.

24 Cut two more strips of fabric that are 3" wide and as wide as your quilt top, including the strips added in Step 23. Sew these strips to the top and bottom of the quilt with the *right* sides together at a ¼" seam allowance. Press the seams open.

The Quilt Backing

Once you've pressed all your seams, you should lay the quilt out very smoothly somewhere and get a finished measurement on it. This is the measurement that your backing will need to be, plus 4 inches in each direction. If you are sending the quilt out to be professionally quilted, then they will tell you specifically how large to cut the backing. The following instructions for the backing are based on you finishing the quilt yourself.

25 Cut one length of backing fabric 8 inches longer than the length of your quilt.

26 Cut another piece of fabric the same size as the last. Then fold that piece lengthwise and press a crease in the fold. Cut the fabric in half lengthwise on the fold.

27 With the *right* sides together, pin and sew the narrow side pieces onto the center piece one at a time with a ½" seam allowance. Press open.

28 Lay the backing out, *wrong* side facing up, tape to a clean floor edge. Then unroll the batting onto the quilt back smoothly. Trim the batting to be the same size as the backing.

29 Lay the quilt top on top of the batting, *right* side facing up in the center, and smooth it out. Pin through all three layers with either curved quilting safety pins or regular safety pins. Pin in several places, such as all the block corners. It's also a good idea to take some long passes of basting stitches both vertically and horizontally through all the layers.

The Quilting Bee

There are a few different methods that one can use to quilt these layers together. Chapter 5 describes how to perform a simple straight stitch, which is essentially the method for hand quilting. Let a quilting friend teach you a good technique for a confidence boost. There is also a hand-tying method, which is not too much more difficult than tacking the quilt in several places with some hand stitches, then hand tying the ends of your thread and trimming. There are particular threads that are ideal for both of these methods however, so check your local quilt shop for advice.

The Binding

After your quilting is complete, trim the backing and batting the same size as the quilt top. Using the bias strips, refer to the section, "Be Edge-y," in Chapter 4 to make the binding on your quilt.

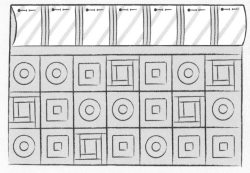

Step 22

Step 27

Chapter 9

Domesticate

Full Contact Cooking Apron

Oh, the messes you make! Don't stain your clothes or your style! Be ready for full contact in the kitchen, and protect your fancy cocktail dress from shoulder to knee. This apron features so many charming details that you could hide a T-shirt and jeans behind it and forego the fancy dress altogether.

Supplies

FABRIC

1 yard for the apron top and skirt

½ yard for the pocket and ties

1½ yards for the bias strips, waistband, and neck strap

Metal buttons for covering (desired size)

Craft paper

Craft scissors

Fabric scissors or rotary cutter and mat

Tape measure

Tailor's chalk

Hand-sewing needle

MY COLOR NOTES

Even though I chose a floral print for this apron, it conjures up cupcakes, sprinkles, cherries, and other food-y thoughts. I used the palette of that floral print to determine my accent fabrics—the polka dots refer to the red speckles on the white flowers, while the subtler red pinstripe finishes the edges with interest.

Cut

1 Cut out patterns **20B** and **20C** from Pattern Page 5, **20A** from Pattern Page 6, and **20A** (continuation) from Pattern Page 7 with craft scissors. Tape the two sections for **20A** together, as instructed on the pattern.

2 For the top piece, cut a square of fabric in one of the following sizes.

Small: 11" x 11"   Medium: 12" x 12"   Large: 13" x 13"

Note: Depending on how tall you are or where you want the top of the apron and waistline to rest, you may not want to cut a perfect square. For instance, if you are shorter in the waist, you may cut a piece that is 12" wide but only 11" tall. The top corners of this piece should rest an inch or two below your collarbone and to the inside of your shoulders. The bottom edge of this piece should reach your navel. The finished top piece will not decrease in width, and only ⅝" in length once the apron is sewn.

3 Cut one apron skirt using pattern piece **20A**, adding any length you wish to the pattern with craft paper. Be sure to mark notches 1, 2, and the center line on the fold of the fabric with a tiny snip, or chalk mark. If you want to increase or decrease the apron skirt's width, simply place the center line edge of the pattern farther away from the fabric fold. You can also fold it to make it smaller. (Remember that since you are cutting on a fold, if you place the pattern fold edge 1" away from the fold of your fabric, then it will increase the width of the apron skirt by 2", and so on. The converse is also true for folding the pattern to make it smaller.)

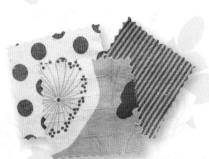

4 Cut two waistband pieces on the fold using pattern piece **20B**. One piece will be the waistband, and one piece will be the waistband facing. Mark notches 1, 2, 3, and the center line with a tiny snip, or chalk mark in the seam allowance. If you are increasing or decreasing the apron skirt, you'll need to do the same with the waistband and facing by the same amount, and in the same manner as in Step 3, by either folding to decrease or moving the fold edge away from the fabric fold to increase it.

5 Cut four waistband backs using pattern piece **20C**. Cut two on the *right* side of the fabric and two on the *wrong* side of the fabric. Mark notch 3 with a tiny snip, or chalk mark in the seam allowance.

6 Cut one rectangle for the pocket measuring 9" x 13" (or whatever size you wish).

7 Cut two apron ties measuring 4" x 25".

8 Cut and join as many 2" wide bias strips as necessary to make a length of bias for trim that is about 3½ yards long. This could vary some, depending on how much you increase or decrease the size of the pattern. You can use the "Maybe I'm Bias" steps in Chapter 4 for tips on how to cut and join bias strips.

9 Cut two neck pieces 4" in width by your desired length. You'll want to determine the length and width of this piece, depending on the final fit of the apron and the size of buttons you use. You should therefore wait until Step 41 to cut and sew this piece.

Sewing the Details

10 Fold the top piece in half lengthwise with the *right* sides together, and pin it in place. At one end, mark a line 1" away from the fold and a length of 2". Sew on this line, stopping at the 2" mark, and backstitching at the beginning and end. This creates an inverted pleat.

11 Open the folded top piece and press the inverted pleat you made in Step 10 so that the seam allowance is evenly dispersed on each side of the seam.

12 Fold one edge of the bias strip ½" back toward the *wrong* side, and press along the entire length of the bias strip.

13 You will now attach bias edging to the three sides of the apron top that do not include the side with the inverted pleat. With the *right* sides together and starting at the bottom of the top piece, align the unfolded edge of the bias strip with the edge of the top piece, and begin sewing with a ½" seam allowance. Stop ½" away from the edge at the corner and backstitch.

14 Fold the strip perpendicularly away from the top piece, creating a 45-degree angled fold in the strip. Then fold it back again over itself, creating a fold that is in line with the edge that you had sewn. (This is similar to the steps for binding a quilt described in "Be Edge-y" in Chapter 4.)

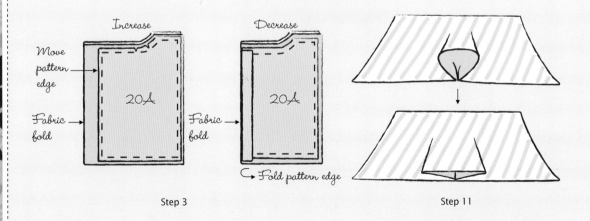

Step 3   Step 11

15 Now begin sewing along this edge, beginning ½" away from the edge, starting and ending with a backstitch and stopping ½" away from the next edge.

16 Repeat Step 14 at this corner.

17 Continue sewing the bias strip on the third side of the apron top, starting ½" away from the edge and sewing all the way to the end, and beginning and ending with a backstitch. Clip the excess bias strip off at the end.

18 From the *right* side of the apron top, turn the bias over the seam allowance, and then fold over onto the *wrong* side so that the folded edge of the bias meets the stitching line. Pin it in place.

19 At the corners, you'll notice when you turn the bias strip back toward the *wrong* side that a nice mitered corner has been formed. You can also create this same mitered corner on the back side. With the back of the apron top facing you, fold down the binding to meet the stitch line and smooth this fold all the way beyond the edge. This will make the bias strip form an angled fold at the corner. Simply turn this angle back in toward the *wrong* side of the apron top to meet the next side's stitching, and you will have formed the mitered corner. Pin it in place.

20 Once all the bias strip edges and corners are pinned in place, topstitch them just about ⅛" away from the inside edge of the bias, while also maintaining an equal distance from the stitch line, around the three sides.

21 Gather between notches 1 and 2 on both sides of the apron skirt's top edge. You can either use your sewing machine's gathering foot with a seam allowance of ½", or refer to the section, "A Small Gathering," in Chapter 4. Gather the fabric enough so that the beginning and ending of the gather points match up with notch 1 and "finished 2" notch on the apron skirt pattern.

22 Edge the sides and bottom of the apron skirt with the remaining bias strip in the same manner as you did with the apron top in Steps 13 through 20.

23 Fold down one of the long edges of the pocket ¼" toward the *wrong* side, then again ¼", and press. Topstitch this rolled hem. This will be the pocket top.

24 Now fold in the sides and bottom in the same manner as Step 23; press and pin it in place.

25 Find the center line nip of the apron skirt and fold half lengthwise, and pin the center mark in a few places on the fold. Do the same with the pocket—at the top and bottom edge.

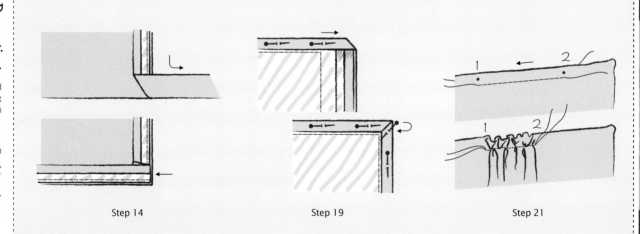

Step 14   Step 19   Step 21

26 With the *wrong* side of the pocket against the *right* side of the apron skirt, lay the pocket on the apron skirt, matching up their center lines. Position the top (topstitched) edge of the pocket roughly 5" or 6" from the top edge of the apron skirt. Carefully slip the pocket edge pins out and back through, to also pin through the apron skirt, one at a time, all the way around the pocket. Do the same by pinning the center line of the pocket to the apron skirt.

27 Now topstitch the pocket all around the sides and bottom in one continuous stitch, ¼" from the edge of the pocket, beginning and ending with a backstitch. At the corners, leave the needle down in the layers of fabric, ¼" away from the edge of the pocket, lift the presser foot, turn the fabric 90 degrees, lower the presser foot, and continue stitching.

28 Fold one of the apron ties in half lengthwise, and press. Cut at a 45-degree angle at the end, with the point of the angle on the fold.

29 Sew the tie down the long side and angled side, with a ½" seam allowance. Clip the corner on the seam allowance and trim the seam allowance on the angled side. Turn the *right* side out and press. Repeat on the other tie.

Assemble the Apron

30 With the *right* sides together, sew two of the waistband back pieces to the ends of the waistband, matching notch 3 and with a ⅜" seam allowance. Repeat with the remaining waistband back pieces and the waistband facing. Press open all seams.

31 Fold and press the long, straight edge of the waistband facing toward the *wrong* side ⅜", and press.

32 Lay out the waistband with the *right* side facing up, and with the curved bottom edge on top. Lay the apron skirt on top with the *wrong* side facing up, roughly aligning notches 1 and 2. Now lay the waistband facing piece *wrong* side facing up with the curved bottom edge on top. Pin all three layers together, matching up notches 1 and 2, thereby sandwiching the apron skirt between the *right* sides of the waistband and waistband facing. You should also have a bit of waistband excess on each end.

33 Sew through all three layers the entire length of the waistband with a ⅜" seam allowance, carefully following the curved edge consistently.

34 Fold the waistband, waistband facing, and all seam allowances up away from the skirt, and press the seam from both sides.

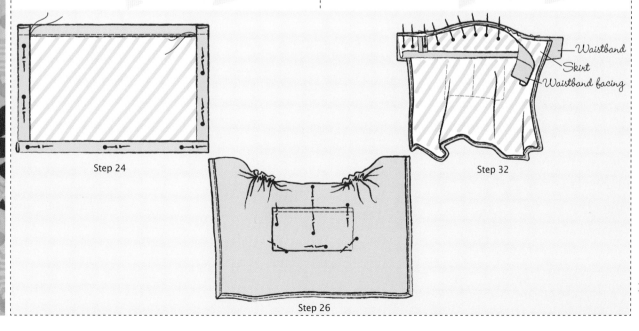

Step 24

Waistband
Skirt
Waistband facing

Step 32

Step 26

35 With the *right* sides together, align the inverted pleat seam of the top piece with the center line of the waistband, and sew with a ⅝" seam allowance.

36 Lay one of the ties between the *right* sides of the waistband and waistband facing, aligning all of the end edges, and fitting the tie snugly up against the waistband seam. Pin it in place. Repeat on the other end with the remaining tie.

37 Sew across the waistband's end with a ⅝" seam allowance, turning at the bottom corner ⅝" away from the edge, and sewing about an inch or so along the top edge of the waistband. Be sure that once you've turned, you are only encasing the tie and not sewing through it, but only sewing through the waistband and waistband facing. Repeat on the other side with the other tie.

38 Clip the corners and pull the ties to turn the waistband ends *right* side out. Press well, and also press down the top edge of the waistband, ⅝" toward the *wrong* side, so that it's in line with the waistband facing.

39 Pin together through all layers, aligning all waistband and waistband facing edges, and encasing all seam allowances. Topstitch the entire perimeter of the waistband ¼" away from its edge. Press the front and back well.

40 Try on the apron. Pin the top corners to your shirt, and tie it at the waist. Take a tape measure and measure the distance from one top corner, around the back of your neck and onto the opposite corner of your apron top. Let the tape measure overlap the apron top by about 2" on each side. Make note of this measurement here: ____.

41 If you haven't done so already, cut out two bias neck straps in a width determined by your button size and a length that is 1" longer that your measurement from Step 40.

Note: I recommend that you cut the strap 1" wider than your buttons. So in the apron shown, the buttons are 2" and I cut the straps 3" wide.

With the *right* sides together, sew around the perimeter of the neck strap with a ¼" seam allowance. Leave a few inches open on one side to turn the *right* side out. Clip the corners. Turn the *right* side out and press.

42 Topstitch around the entire perimeter of the neck strap ⅛" away from the edge. Pin the strap in place on both sides, overlapping the top edges of the apron.

Note: While it's just pinned, try it on to be sure you can slip it on comfortably over your head. If it's too tight to slip on, you'll want to make one of the buttons functional and the other decorative and permanently attached to the apron.

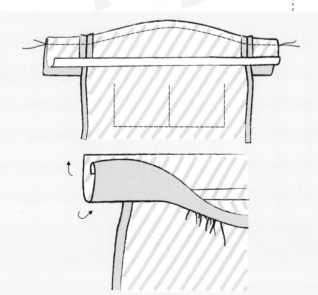

Steps 34

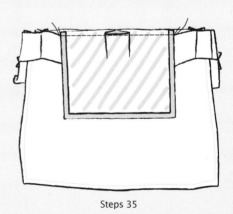

Steps 35

43 Stitch the straps down with overlapping horizontal and vertical lines of stitching to tack them in place. Make sure your stitching will be hidden by the size of your buttons.

44 Sew the buttons in place by hand. Make cherry vanilla cupcakes at once.

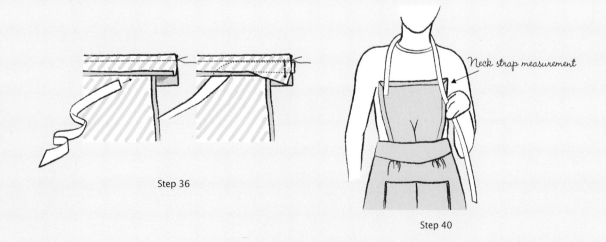

Step 36

Neck strap measurement

Step 40

Cup Half Full Apron

Ahh, optimism. It's the grace-saving quality whispering in your ear that you'll only spill something on the bottom half of yourself while you're in the kitchen. Whether that's a realistic notion or not, this little apron pays homage to optimism with a simple but flattering design and with little cup-shaped pockets.

Supplies

FABRIC

⅜ yard of 44/45" cotton for apron

1½ yard contrasting fabric for waistband and bias strips for edging

¼ yard for pockets

2½" x 23" of lightweight, non-fusible interfacing

Fabric scissors or rotary cutter and mat

Craft scissors

Tailor's chalk

Yardstick

MY COLOR NOTES

I love the drip lines in this fabric print and thought it was playfully perfect for a little café-style apron. The waistband-and-trim fabric has a different style and scale of tear shapes and lines. I chose orange for the pockets to pop against the mostly white fabric and to complement the blue trim.

Cut

1   Cut out patterns **21A** from Pattern Page 8 and **21B** from Pattern Page 7 with craft scissors.

2   Cut one of pattern piece **21A** from the apron fabric on the lengthwise fold.

3   Cut four of pattern piece **21B** from the pocket fabric. You may want the inner pocket fabric to be different than the outer pocket, in which case you should cut two of pattern piece **21B** from each.

4   Cut a bias strip measuring 2" in width by 65" in length. (For tips on cutting and joining bias strips, see the sections, "Maybe I'm Bias" and "Be Edge-y," in Chapter 4.)

Note: If you choose to make the apron front wider or longer than the pattern, you'll need to increase the length of your strip by as much.

5   To calculate the length that your waistband ties should be, add 40" to your waist measurement and write the result here_____. Cut a piece from your waistband and fabric that is this measurement in length and and 6" in width. (It's fine to join pieces to form this long strip; just sew them *right* sides together, with a ½" seam allowance, and press open the seams.)

6   Cut a rectangle from the lightweight interfacing, measuring 2½" x 23".

Prepare the Apron Body

7   After folding the apron body in half lengthwise with the *right* sides together, pin the fabric or mark with a chalk line at the "inverted pleat" mark, as shown on the pattern piece, making note of the stopping point, as well.

8   Straight-stitch the fabric together on the "inverted pleat" line with the *right* sides together, backstitching at the beginning and end to secure it.

9 With the *wrong* side facing up, press the large seam allowance from the inverted pleat down at the top, equally distributing the seam allowance on either side of the box pleat seam. (See Step 11 in the "Full Contact Cooking Apron" project.)

10 With the apron body facing up, lay the apron pattern on top as you line up the outer edges. Fold down the pattern at the top of the pocket placement line and pin the fabric *right* at that line. Unfold the pattern. Now fold the pattern in the other direction at the outside edge of the pocket placement line and pin the fabric at that line. Flip the pattern over and repeat this sequence on the other side so that you've marked the outer corners for each of the pockets. (You can also do this with chalk if you prefer.)

Attach the Pockets

11 With the *right* sides of one inner and one outer pocket together, pin and sew along the sides and curved bottom of the pocket in one continuous line at a ½" seam allowance. Sew carefully around the curved edge to maintain an even seam allowance. Setting the machine to a shorter stitch length will help keep your curved seams smooth. Leave the top open.

12 Clip wedges out of the curved seam allowance. Turn the pocket *right* side out, pressing out the inner seam with your finger as you do so.

13 Smooth out the curved edges and press on both sides. Turn the open top edges inward and press down ½". Topstitch along the top edge ¼" from the edge, backstitching at the beginning and end. Press.

14 Repeat Steps 11, 12, and 13 on the other pocket.

15 With the inner pocket side and *right* side of the apron together, align the outer corner of one of the pockets with the corner markings that you made in Step 10. Pin the pocket in place, pointing the pins from the inside of the pocket toward the edges. Repeat this step on the other pocket.

16 Starting at the top edge, topstitch the pocket ¼" from its edge. Continue around the bottom and up to the top of the other side. Backstitch at the beginning and end to secure. Repeat this step on the other pocket.

Note: You may want to switch to a slightly heavier-duty machine needle because you will be sewing through several layers of fabric when you stitch the pockets in place.

Add the Edging and Waistband

17 With the bias strip made from Step 4, press back ½" of the strip toward the *wrong* side, all along the long edge of the strip.

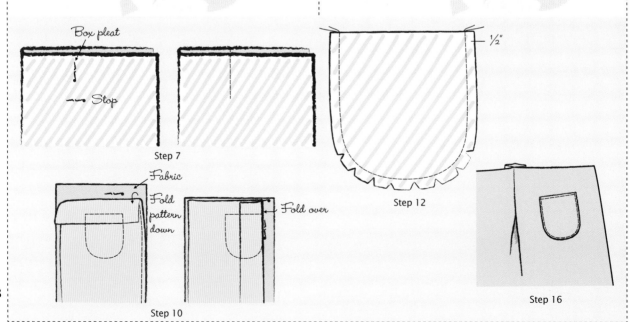

Box pleat

Stop

Step 7

Fabric

Fold pattern down

Fold over

Step 12

½"

Step 10

Step 16

18 With the *right* sides together and starting at the top *right* of the apron (your right as it faces you), align the apron's edge with the edge of the bias strip that is not pressed back. Begin sewing the bias strip to the apron with a ½" seam allowance. Continue around, ending at the top of the left side of the apron.

Note: I find the above step much easier to do without pinning, because the bias strip will give a little differently than the fabric that was cut on the grain. Therefore, where it ends up as you sew it may not be where you pin it. So you'll just continue to reposition the edges as you are sewing, while maintaining a consistent seam allowance. Do try to prevent the bias strip from stretching out too much as you sew it to the apron.

19 Bluntly trim off any excess bias strip that extends beyond the apron top. Press the edging seam just from the front.

20 Wrap the folded edge of the bias strip back around the seam allowance and toward the *wrong* side of the apron. Line up the folded edge along the edging seam and pin in a few places.

21 With the *wrong* side of apron facing up, topstitch the bias strip down just about ⅛" from the inside folded edge. Press on both sides.

22 Fold the waistband cut in Step 5 in half lengthwise, and press a crease along the whole length. Also, keeping the waistband folded, trim each end at a 45-degree angle.

23 Find the center point of the waistband (folding in half is an easy way), and mark it with a pin or a chalk line.

24 After you find the center point of the interfacing piece you made in Step 6, lay the interfacing inside the *wrong* side of the waistband along the inner fold, lining up with the center point of the waistband. Pin through only the interfacing and one side of the fabric.

25 Machine-baste the interfacing in place along both long edges to the inside of the waistband. This will be the waistband back side.

26 Fold the waistband lengthwise up the other way with the *right* sides together to align the edges. Pin the waistband closed, starting 2" away from the end of the interfacing and toward the angled end of the strap. Sew together with a ½" seam allowance, taking a turn at the angled corner and finishing at the end with a backstitch. Repeat on the other side.

27 Clip the corners of the pointed ends and trim the seam allowance on the angle. Turn the straps *right* side out and press well on both sides.

28 With the *right* sides together, align the edge of the waistband front with the top edge of the apron. You should be centering the apron within the interfaced part of the waistband. Pin just through the waistband front and apron.

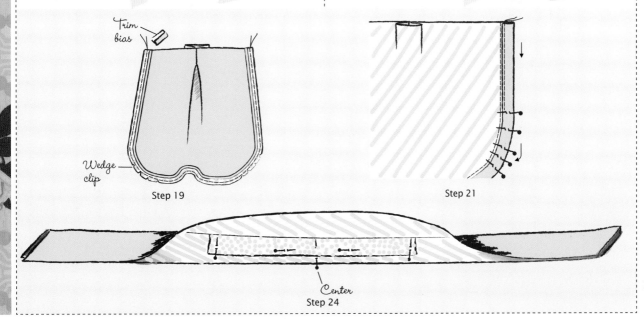

Trim bias

Wedge clip

Step 19

Step 21

Center
Step 24

29 Sew the waistband front to the apron, backstitching at the beginning and end. Press all seam allowances up within the waistband, at the same time folding the waistband back seam allowance up around the interfacing.

30 Pin the folded bottom edge of the waistband back just to the inside of the waistband seam. With the *wrong* side of the apron facing up, begin topstitching at the bottom of the waistband ⅛" from the edge of the waistband. Continue topstitching on the entire perimeter of the waistband and straps until you end at the beginning point, and backstitch to secure it. Press the entire apron well.

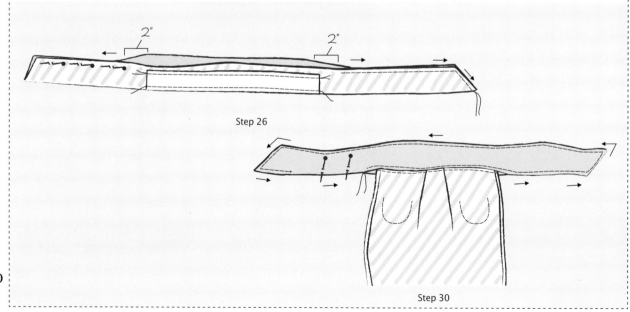

2"

2"

Step 26

Step 30

Here's the Dish Towel

Making these little dish towels is something to keep you still for awhile and sharpen your skills in appliqué and embroidery. If you find the time investment a bit more than you'd like to spend on something that will dry your hands at the kitchen sink, feel free to adapt these same designs and techniques to a table runner, placemats, or even a pillow or tote bag. Or just hang the fancy new dish towels too high for anyone to reach them.

Supplies

FABRIC

¾ yard of 44–45"-thick, loose-weave cotton

or

2 plain pre-made towels

Assorted scrap cotton fabric for appliqué design

Trim fabric measuring 3" x 17"

Two-sided lightweight, fusible interfacing (optional)

Poster board (p)

Hand appliqué or quilting needles

Hand-embroidery needle

Embroidery floss

Embroidery hoop

Fabric scissors or rotary cutter and mat

Craft scissors

Yardstick

Aluminum foil

MY COLOR NOTES

Since I went with a printed fabric as the towel, I chose one that was only one color of print on a neutral ground. This way, there is still room to make the embellishments stand out, by choosing scraps in colors that complement the background fabric.

Cut

1 Cut out patterns **22A**, **22B**, **22C**, **22D**, **22E**, **22F**, **22Ap**, **22Bp**, **22Cp**, **22Dp**, **22Ep**, and **22Fp** from Pattern Page 7 with craft scissors.

2 Cut a rectangle from the fabric measuring 17" x 27", taking the 27" measurement from the length of the fabric in line with the selvedge.

Make the Towel

3 At ½" from each side of one corner on a short end, press down a small dog-ear toward the *wrong* side. Repeat this on the opposing corner of the towel.

4 Now roll back the edge of that end ¼" twice, and pin it in place. Roll back both of the long sides in the same manner, and pin. You should now have two nice mitered corners for hemming.

5 Hem the three pinned sides with a straight stitch on the machine as close to the inside folded edge as possible. Press.

6 With the trim fabric, press back one long side ¼" toward the *wrong* side.

Trim the Towel

7 With *right* sides together, align the un-pressed long edge of the trim fabric with the un-hemmed edge of the towel, and pin in place. Snugly wrap the trim fabric ends that extend beyond the towel around to the *wrong* side of the towel, and pin in place.

8 Sew the trim fabric to the towel using a straight stitch and ½" seam allowance, backstitching at the beginning and end.

9 Turn the trim fabric down to show the *right* side, and press all seam allowances toward the bottom.

10 Now fold the bottom pressed edge of the trim fabric back up toward the *wrong* side of the towel, keeping the trim fabric ends folded in, and align the bottom folded edge just below the stitch line you made in Step 8. Pin in place.

11 Topstitch the trim down as close to the folded edge as possible, trying also to maintain a consistent distance from the other stitch line. (You could also whip-stitch or blind-stitch the trim in place, passing your needle only through the seam allowances to anchor the trim's edge.) Press again.

Prepare the Embellishments

For all practical purposes, you now have yourself a dish towel! If you'd like to add some nostalgic details, however, keep on going with the following steps. The two appliqué patterns and embroidery designs are just offered as suggestions, but feel free to get creative here. Arrange and combine these elements any way you wish, or maybe include a family monogram or some spare buttons here and there.

12 For the Wildflower design, you will make one fabric yo-yo. For the Growing Garden design, you can make as many as desired. Make fabric yo-yos from a 4½" circle of fabric. You can use the directions in the "Opposites Attract" project in Chapter 6 (see page 74), but eliminate the cardboard center from the directions.

13 For the Wildflower design, using the patterns, cut out six of **22A**, six of **22B**, and six of **22C** from fabric scraps. Also cut one each of **22Ap**, **22Bp**, and **22Cp** from poster board. For the Growing Garden design, cut as many leaves from **22D**, **22E**, and **22F**. Cut one each of **22Dp**, **22Ep**, and **22Fp** from poster board. Mark all the poster board pieces with an X on their *right* sides.

Note: Steps 14 and 15 detail how to fold back the edges of the appliqué pieces. If you are familiar with how to do needle-turn appliqué with or without freezer paper, you can use that method instead of the following.

14 Using the "Super Circles" technique on page 57, press back the edges of your petal shapes around the poster-board template, then wrap the foil around the fabric and press, one by one, to prepare them to be sewn down. Be sure that you place the side of the poster board with the X on it against the *wrong* side of your fabric as you press the edges around it.

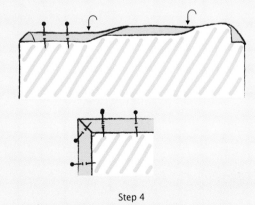

Step 4

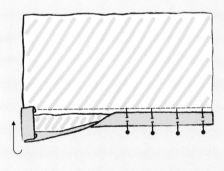

Step 10

15 Optional: I sometimes cut small pieces of very lightweight, double-sided, fusible interfacing just barely smaller than the poster-board template. Just remove one side of the backing paper and press against the *wrong* side of the appliqué piece after you've pressed back its edges. Be sure to keep the interfacing side against the fabric piece, and the remaining backing paper side against the iron. This helps to hold the folds in place. Leave the other backing paper on for now.

16 With the *wrong* sides together, fold your towel in half lengthwise, then again crosswise, and place a pin at the very center point of the towel through the top layer. Open your towel again and lay it out in front of you, *right* side facing you.

17 In the area of the towel between the center pin and the bottom trim, and using the figures on the next page as a guide, lay out your appliqué pieces in your desired arrangement. Keep in mind that when you fold and hang your towel, usually only the bottom half and the center third of the towel are visible. Pin the pieces in place. If you've put fusible

interfacing on the pieces, you can eliminate the need for pins by pressing the pieces in place after you've removed the remaining backing paper.

Appliqué the Pieces and Embroider

The next portion of this project is to be savored, and perhaps completed over time. Piece by piece, you can stitch the design onto the towel using the technique described in the section, "Sewing Blind," in Chapter 5 (the section, "An Invisible Variation," in Chapter 5 is also particularly helpful). Press the towel again after you've finished the appliqué work.

You can now begin to embellish the design further with embroidery floss. In the Wildflower design, I used both split stitches and French knots. In the Growing Garden design, I used running stitches and French knots. In all cases, I used all six strands of the embroidery floss and a nice, sharp embroidery needle. Be sure to read about some of these techniques in Chapter 5, in the "Simply Stitch-y" section. The figures on the next page point out a few characteristics and the direction of stitches for the two towel designs.

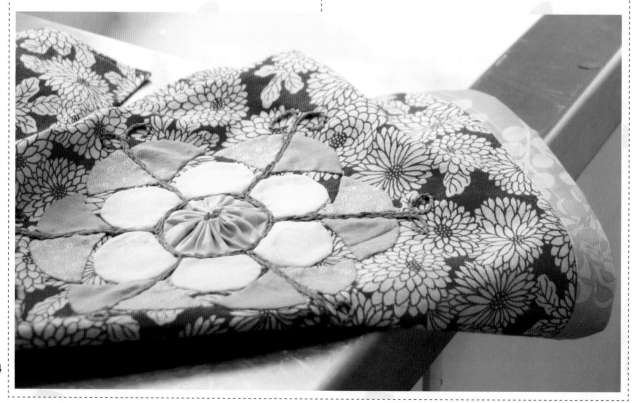

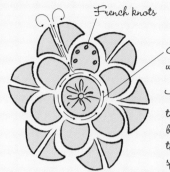

French knots

Go around yo-yo once with split stitch.

Then go through petals to make curley-q's and back down and around the yo-yo to the next space between petals.

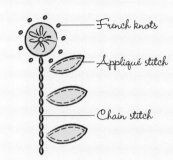

French knots

Appliqué stitch

Chain stitch

Wildflower layout

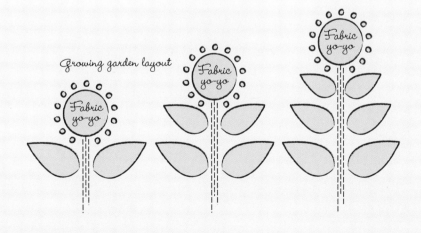

Growing garden layout

For Kicks Patchwork Ball

Pardon the blatant intrusion of geometry while we're having fun, but it's quite necessary to make this darling little patchwork ball. This is a perfect baby gift project that will use up a lot of those small scraps that are hard to find other uses for. While it's great for babies, I know a few school-age boys who are not too grown up to kick this patchy ball up and down our hallway.

Supplies

FABRIC

Fabric scraps

Fiberfill

Rotary cutter and mat (highly recommended)

Craft scissors

Quilting needle

MY COLOR NOTES

I went all out on this little ball using bright and fancy fabrics in candy colors that would entrance any baby's sweet eyes for hours. If you want the traditional soccer ball design, just cut all the pentagons from one solid color and all the hexagons from another solid color. It would also be fun to use various textured fabrics, like corduroy, to entertain baby's curious little fingers.

Cut

1   Cut out patterns **23A** and **23B** from Pattern Page 9 with craft scissors.

2   Trace the pentagon (**23A**) and hexagon (**23B**) templates above onto paper.

3   Cut 20 fabric hexagons using the hexagon template.

4   Cut 12 fabric pentagons using the pentagon template.

Assemble the Pieces

For all machine sewing, use a straight stitch with ¼" seam allowance, and with *right* sides together. Also use a pretty short stitch length. These are small pieces, and so if your machine has a speed setting, you may want to slow it down. Attach new pieces from left to right around the ball and always keep the piece that you are adding on top with its *wrong* side facing you as you go. Try practicing the piecing technique in the first few steps before using your final fabric pieces.

5 Starting at one side of a pentagon, sew one side of a hexagon, starting and ending ¼" away from the edge and backstitching at the beginning and end.

6 Open the two pieces to their *right* sides and attach another hexagon to one side of the pentagon (a) and to the next side of the other hexagon, sort of in an "L" stitch line (b). To do this, you will begin stitching the hexagon and pentagon sides together ¼" away from the edge, stopping at the seam you made in Step 5, putting the machine needle down, lifting the presser foot, aligning the second side of the hexagon to the other hexagon, putting the foot down, and continuing, stopping ¼" away from the edge.

7 Repeat Step 6 twice, adding two more hexagons to the edges of the pentagon and to the hexagon beside it.

8 Join the fifth hexagon to the last side of the pentagon in the same manner as above, but also continue to sew on a third side to close the ring of hexagons. You should now have what looks like a flower shape with one pentagon in the center, and five hexagons as the petals.

9 Add a row of five pentagons above the hexagons, one each in the space formed by the hexagons.

10 Next add a row of hexagons between the pentagons, one each in the space formed by the pentagons and hexagons from the previous row. You will, however, be joining each of the hexagons of three sides.

11 Add another row of hexagons, one each in the space formed above the pentagons and between the hexagons from the last step. You will also be joining each of these hexagons on three sides.

12 Now add a row of five pentagons, one each in the spaces formed by the hexagons. You will be joining the pentagons on three of their sides.

13 To begin adding the final row of five hexagons in the space between the last pentagons, join the first hexagon on three sides between two of the pentagons.

14 The three subsequent hexagons will first join one of their sides to the previous hexagon sewn on and then three more sides, for a total of four sides joined in one stitch line.

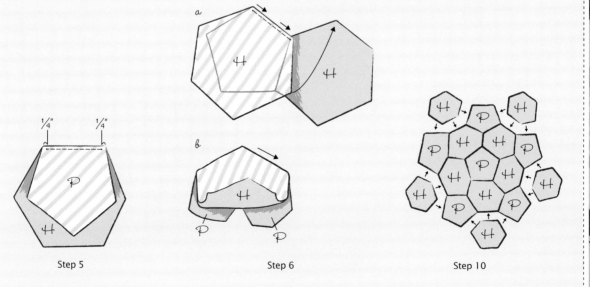

Step 5   Step 6   Step 10

15 On the last hexagon in this row, only join the first four sides of it and leave the fifth side between it and the first hexagon from Step 13 open.

16 Using what should be your last pentagon, join it on three sides only to those three hexagons that do not have a seam left open.

Stuff and Finish the Ball

17 Fold the two open edges of the last pentagon back toward the *wrong* side, and hand-baste them with a ¼" seam allowance.

18 On only one of the hexagons, fold back toward the *wrong* side the edge that meets the other hexagon, and hand-baste it with a ¼" seam allowance.

19 Stuff the ball with fiberfill only small amounts at a time, gradually pressing it out on all sides to evenly disperse the stuffing. The ball should be quite full to maintain plumpness after it has been played with for a while.

20 A well-stuffed ball will cause the opening to stay spread out, but with a little work you will be able to shut the opening. Take a straight pin and insert it partway through the basted edge of the hexagon; then, using the pin, pull the hexagon into place over the flat seam allowance of the hexagon next to it, and push the pin down through both. Add pins on this edge to hold the seam in place.

21 Now insert a straight pin partway into the point of the basted pentagon, and pull it over the seam between the hexagons and push all the way down through the layers. Add pins to both edges of the basted pentagon to position it correctly.

22 With a quilting needle and thread, you can now close the openings. Refer to "Sewing Blind" in Chapter 5 for instructions on how to close a seam. Remove the hand basting when you are finished.

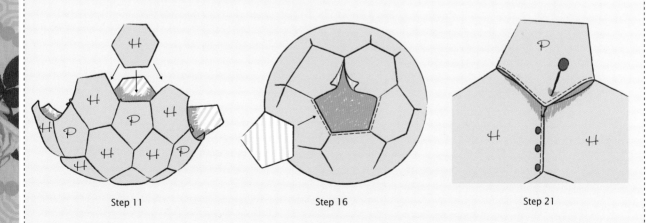

Step 11   Step 16   Step 21

Doggie Dreams Bed

How could we spruce up the house and not include a soft spot for puppers? This cozy dog bed is a simple cushion with a zippered cover that you can customize, based on your best friend's size. An inner cover layered with waterproofing spray keeps the mattress fresh, while the zippered outer cover is easily removed for washing. A cozy dog is a happy dog.

Supplies

FABRIC

The amount of all fabrics will vary, depending on bed size:

- Lightweight cotton fabric like broadcloth for inner cover
- Medium- to heavyweight cotton fabric for outer cover top and bottom
- Light- to medium-weight cotton for contrast piping
- Light- to medium-weight cotton fabric for outer sides

Foam cushion at least 4" or 5" thick

1 zipper as long as the longest side of the bed, plus about 8" (a zipper sold by the yard is a good option)

Cording for piping in desired thickness (length should be the perimeter of the bed × 2, plus a few inches)

Fabric scissors or rotary cutter and mat

Hand-sewing needle

Yardstick

Water repellant spray

1 dog

MY COLOR NOTES

As silly as it sounds, I chose a fabric that my yellow lab King Leo would look cute on. I was also completely smitten with this little bunny fabric and thought he should have daily non-tragic encounters with bunnies (bad dog!). So going with the playful dreams theme, I also chose a contrast fabric for the sides depicting little bumblebees. Leo is thoroughly amused by real bumblebees, and I'd like to think he'll be charmed by little fabric bees. (I'm dreaming too now, I imagine.)

Determine the Cushion Size

The most straightforward way to decide how big the dog bed should be is to observe *your* pup's sleeping habits. Roughly measure out a rectangle of space around your precious pet while he's sleeping, leaving as much room around him that you feel would keep him cozy. Make note of the length (or long side) and width (or short side), and head to your local sewing center to find a foam cushion. Most large fabric store chains carry foam in a variety of thicknesses sold by the foot or yard. While you may have to buy a greater width than you need, they can usually cut it down to the exact dimensions you'll need for the bed.

Once you have the cushion cut to its final size, write the dimensions below for your reference in cutting the other materials.

Length = _____ Width = _____ Height (thickness) = _____

Cut and Make the Inner Cover

1 Cut two rectangles from the inner cover fabric in a length that is equal to the cushion length plus 2", and a width that is equal to the cushion width plus 2". This will be the inner top and inner bottom.

2 Cut two rectangles from the inner cover fabric in a length that is equal to the cushion length plus 2", and a width that is equal to the cushion height plus 2". These will be the inner long sides.

3 Cut two rectangles from the inner cover fabric in a length that is equal to the cushion width plus 2", and a width that is equal to the cushion height plus 2". These will be the inner short sides.

Note: All the sewing should include backstitching at the beginning and end to secure it.

4 With the *right* sides together, attach the inner top to one of the inner long sides with their edges aligned starting and ending ½" away from the edges, and with a ½" seam allowance. Repeat on the other side with the other inner long side.

5 Open these sides out so that all the *right* sides will face up, and press the seams from the *right* side.

6 With the *right* sides together, sew the inner short side to the short side of the inner top, aligning their edges, starting and stopping 2½" away from the edges and with a ½" seam allowance. (Where you stop and start sewing on this piece should be right in the seams made from Step 4.) Repeat on the opposite short side.

7 With the *right* sides together, sew the short sides of the inner bottom piece to the inner short sides, starting and stopping ½" away from the edges and with a ½" seam allowance.

8 On one of the open sides, with the *right* sides together, sew the long side of the inner bottom piece to the inner long side, starting and stopping ½" away from the ends and with a ½" seam allowance.

9 On the same side that was sewn in Step 8, sew the corners of the inner long sides and the inner short sides on each end, starting and stopping ½" away from the edges and with a ½" seam allowance. Make sure that this stitching has completely closed the opening, and also take care not to catch either the bottom piece or the top piece in this seam. You should now have a dimensional rectangle that is open on one long side.

10 Clip the corners off the seam allowances from all six joined corners.

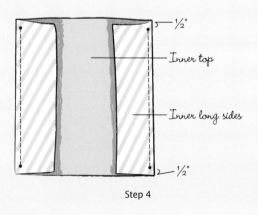

Step 4

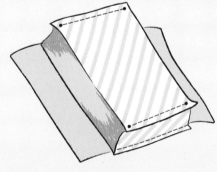

Step 7

11 Turn the cushion *right* side out and insert the cushion. Push the cushion snugly into place, with the corners and edges of the cushion lining up well with the seamed corners and seamed edges of the inner cover.

12 At the open end of the inner cover, fold in the edges of the bottom piece and the inner short side pieces over the edges of the foam. Then fold the three open edges of the inner long side ½", and baste by hand if you wish.

13 Fold up the inner long side, overlapping the bottom and inner short side edges, to meet the corners and edges of the cushion. Insert pins straight into all the layers and the foam cushion to hold them in place, and whip-stitch closed.

14 It would be a good idea to take the covered cushion outdoors and apply an environmentally friendly, water repellant spray to help keep the cushion fresh and dry. You may want to wear a protective mask while spraying. Allow to dry outside.

Cut and Make the Outer Cover

15 Cut two rectangles from the outer cover fabric in a length that is equal to the cushion length plus 2", and a width that is equal to the cushion width plus 2". This will be the outer top and outer bottom.

16 Cut one rectangle from the outer side fabric in a length that is equal to the cushion length plus 2", and a width that is equal to the cushion height plus 2". This will be the outer long side.

17 Cut two rectangles from the outer side fabric in a length that is equal to the cushion width less ½", and a width that is equal to the cushion height plus 2". These will be the outer short sides.

18 Cut two rectangles from the outer side fabric in a length that is equal to the cushion length plus 7" and a width that is equal to half of the cushion height plus 1⅝". Once these two pieces are joined by a zipper, it will be the zippered side.

19 Cut and join as many bias strips as you need from the contrast fabric to make two lengths of piping that are each equal in length to the perimeter of the cushion plus about 5" or 6". Use the sections, "Maybe I'm Bias" and "Pipe Dream," in Chapter 4 for instructions on how to cut bias strips and how to make piping. Once you've made the piping, trim the header on it to about ½" wide from the stitch line. You could also use pre-made piping instead of creating your own.

Note: Don't forget that you'll want to use your zipper foot or cording foot to make the piping, and any other time that you will be sewing alongside the piping.

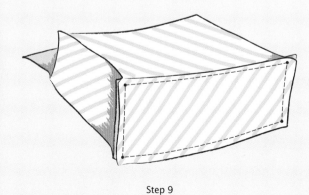

Step 9

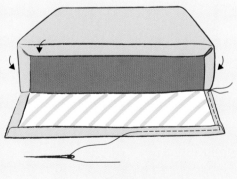

Step 12

20 Attach piping to the *right* side of the outer top, lining up the header edges with the edges of the outer top, using a $^3/_8$" seam allowance. Repeat with the other length of piping on the *right* side of the outer bottom. For some tips on sewing piping into a seam, see the section, "Pipe Dream," in Chapter 4.

21 With the *right* sides together, sew the outer long side to the long edge of the outer top, starting and stopping ½" away from the edges and with a ½" seam allowance. Open and press the seam from the *right* side. Set it aside.

22 With the *right* sides together, machine-baste the length of the two zippered side pieces together with a $^3/_8$" seam allowance. Press open. Follow the instructions from the "Zippity Hoorah: The Centered Zipper" steps in Chapter 4 to install a centered zipper along this seam.

Note: When you topstitch the zipper in place, you can let the topstitching run the entire length of the seam to the ends.

23 Once you've installed the zipper and have removed the basting stitches, move the zipper head down a few inches. Align the very top 1½" of the zipper seam at their folded edges and zigzag together. Backstitch a few times at the end, right above where the zipper head will be, to secure. Also zigzag across the bottom 1½" or so of the zipper seam in the same manner.

24 With the *right* sides together, sew the ends of the zippered side and one of the outer short sides together with a ½" seam allowance, and backstitch at the beginning and end. Repeat with the other outer short side at the other end of the zippered side. Press the seam allowances toward the outer short sides, and topstitch down through all layers ¼" away from the seam.

25 With the joined outer top and outer long side from Step 21, and the joined zippered side and short sides from Step 25, and with *right* sides together using a ½" seam allowance, sew the joined sides along the three open edges of the outer top piece. Begin, turn corners, and end ½" away from the edge, leaving the needle down and raising the presser foot to turn corners. Clip the seam allowance on the two corners.

26 With the *right* sides together, sew the outer bottom to the outer long side along their long edges with a ½" seam allowance, beginning and ending ½" away from the edges.

27 With the *right* sides together, sew the remaining three edges of the outer bottom to the remaining three side edges with a ½" seam allowance, and beginning and ending ½" away from the edges.

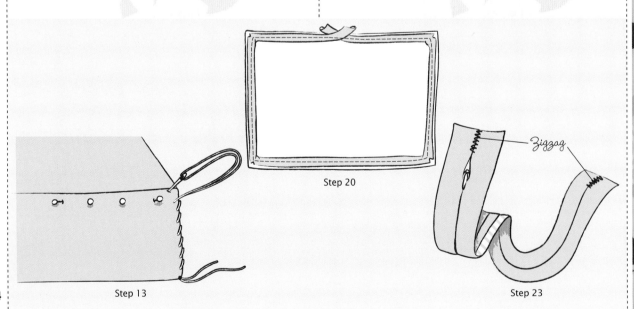

Step 20

Step 13

Step 23

Zigzag

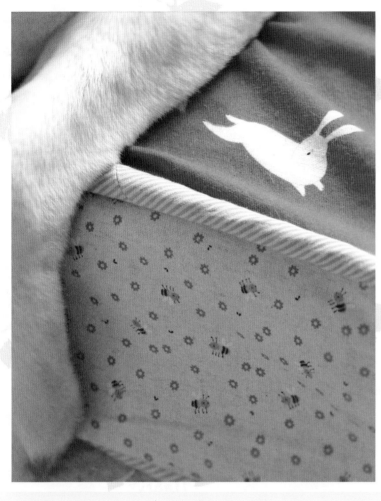

28 Reach through one of the two remaining corner openings to unzip the zipper all the way.

29 Now close the remaining corner openings with a ½" seam allowance and beginning and ending ½" away from the edges. Make sure that this stitching has completely closed the opening, and also take care not to catch either the bottom piece or the top piece in this seam. Clip and snip all the seam allowances at the corners.

30 Turn the cushion cover *right* side out through the open zipper, and insert the cushion. Close the zipper and whistle for the puppy!

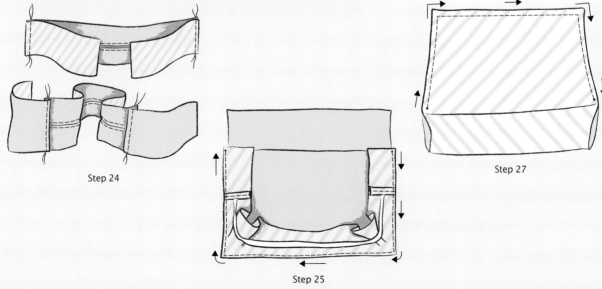

Step 24

Step 25

Step 27

Index